DANCING the GAY LIB BLUES

A Year in the Homosexual Liberation Movement

by Arthur Bell

SIMON AND SCHUSTER
NEW YORK

FIRST PRINTING

SBN 671-21042-4
Library of Congress Catalog Card Number: 78-159124
Designed by Irving Perkins
Manufactured in the United States of America
By H. Wolff Book Mfg. Co., Inc., New York, N.Y.

TO THE STREET PEOPLE

Letter to my editor

DEAR JONATHAN:

You asked me to tell you a bit about what makes up a gay liberationist. I can't. I'll tell you a little about myself, background stuff, a thumbnail, no, a hangnail sketch of a movie-oriented childhood, what went on before I met the man who occupies many pages of this book, and perhaps a freeform line or two, thoughts about liberation.

Let's start with the gay thing. How far back does it go with me? From the time I was three or four, I imagine, maybe earlier, maybe from the time I tripped out of the womb, maybe before that. I remember looking at tall men before I could say Gary Cooper, little lascivious me, goo, wanting a lanky guy like the Sergeant York with wavy blond hair who visited his mother next door. I remember running away to the movies, the Fortway in Brooklyn, flipping over Tarzan and wondering whether he'd drop that loin cloth. I sighed over the sultry sirens—Gene Tierney, Rita Hayworth—and wanted to be like them, beautiful, free, loved, and wicked. On Bay Ridge pavements, I roller-skated—"Look, Vera Hruba Ralston"—and snubbed my nose at the John Wayne/John Payne war games of my male contemporaries and refused to play doctors and nurses with the kids down the block. I traded cut-out pictures from the pages of *Photoplay* with the girls next door.

No football for Arthur—a Gene Tierney scrapbook instead.

My uncle Hi, now dead, took me to *Leave Her to Heaven* when the Roxy had stage shows. We passed the backstage entrance and I got a flicker of two men in rouge flirting with each other. Uncle Hi said they were chorus boys, and three years later I went back with my autograph book in hand and started collecting autographs at the stage door of the Roxy. I think I was looking to be raped, but whatever, nothing happened, except it was glamorous and Vivian Blaine asked me to have an ice-cream soda with her.

No pubic woes for me. I felt free at twelve. I'd skip school and meet my friends at Sardi's or "21" at noon. There was Adaire, a red-headed eleven year old Black (except we said Negress) and Smiley and a M-M-M-Marty who stuttered, and the Secret Six who knew the whereabouts of every Hollywood film star in town. Most of us were homosexuals, too young to define homosexuality or practice it, so we chased stars instead. For a year I followed Katharine Hepburn, who told me she never signed, not even on Christmas Eve. She was my biggest challenge, and I finally got her on a rainy Wednesday, after a matinee of *The Millionairess*. I knew the service stairway at the Waldorf Astoria and climbed thirty-five floors for Barbara Stanwyck, only to be discovered by the house dicks and evicted. This early sleuthing and chasework was to come in handy this past year in newspaper assignments and in gay liberation dealings with political figures.

My family moved to Montreal when I was in junior high. Leaving New York for a city where *Oklahoma* played ten years later, was traumatic. Since there was little celebrity action, I began a letter-writing campaign to movie greats. Miss Jane Wyman, c/o Warner Brothers, Burbank, California (no zip code then). "Dear Miss Wyman, This is a difficult letter to write because I used to be right-handed and my right hand was shot off during the war, so I'm writing to you with my left hand instead. Will you send me a personally autographed photograph of yourself. Sincerely." I still have the photo. "To Sergeant Arthur Bell. Face the future undaunted and unafraid. Sincerely. Jane Wyman."

I was never happy with my rank, and changed from Sergeant to Lieutenant to Flying Officer to Admiral. I think Sophie Tucker sicced the postal authorities on me. There was some nasty business about free record albums to Admiral Arthur Bell held up at Canadian customs. An inspector paid a call on my father one day about fraudulency through the mails. Thereafter I was plain Mister, and the photos that followed were mostly mimeographed by the studio.

My family went through a nouveau riche period during that time, and, in Montreal I went through a period of maladjustment. I believed I was the strangest of all strange creatures. I was a chaste fourteen, I didn't know about sex—either firsthand or explained by charts or textbooks. My mother and father might have been afraid to talk to their exotic son who preferred Vivian Blaine to Casey Stengel. And the stuff that the kids were talking about at school was beyond me.

So I found out about sex my own way. At seventeen. At the Midway Theater, during a lofty Jean Simmons movie. The knee bit, as a starter, then winding up in a two-bit rooming house with an aging gorilla who satisfied my youthful needs and scared the hell out of me. I went

9

into retirement for four months, then emerged at seventeen and a half, wanting chorus boys, getting more gorillas, and finally finding love, I thought, with a young man with a Polish name. I left home and moved into a one-room dump and learned how to cook Jello, creatively mixing flavors (cherry lime is flawless). That wasn't enough to keep it going. I moved back to Mother and Dad, swearing off men and love for life. Unfortunately, a week later, I met someone whom I truly loved, but who didn't love me. For the next two years I wore out my Helen Morgan records. Rejection was the most wonderful, awful thing in the world and I reveled in it. I didn't realize what an ass I was until one day it hurt too deep and I used the hurt as an excuse to leave Montreal for my wonderful New York.

That was ten years ago, and this is all very sketchy, Jonathan, and a million things have happened to me since, one one-hundredth of which have been described in the book. I feel though, that leaving home and hearth and unrequited love when I did was a liberation dance. It was a new beginning, probably my first adult forward thrust. God knows what would have happened had I stayed in Montreal.

My head, of course, has changed considerably since those Gene Tierney/Jane Wyman days. It changed considerably since I entered the gay movement, and considerably more since writing the last line of this book two months ago. It will continue to change. But I don't kid myself any more. At this late stage, those changes are on the fifth level, not the seventh. Neither a weekend with a Roxy chorus boy nor an apology from Sophie Tucker from up above nor a century with homosexual liberation will totally revamp the basic Arthur Bell that was conceived by his father and mother and is a composite of the things he's seen and the people he's met along the road of life. Being a gay activist has shaken my psyche, yes, rearranged it, yes, but changed it completely, never. I can't dance away history and experience.

Still in all, coming out full blast this past year was a great veil drop for me. Putting myself "on the line," proclaiming my homosexuality in klieg lights, opening up to all and sundry became a natural extension of self, and lovely.

On gay liberation, Jonathan, I feel that as more homosexuals drop their veils—fourth or fifth or whatever—there will be a loosening up of the concrete that has been paved upon us, sometimes by ourselves, and hardened. The male will not be ostracized for collecting Dixie Cup covers instead of baseball bats, there'll be less "normal" as defined by The Book of Normal Patterns, subsequently less self-destruction, less blues, more dancing, more liberation, more gay—in every sense of the word.

Coming out is a beginning. Changing straitjacket laws is a beginning. "Zapping" is a beginning. Dancing our way to liberation is a beginning. But only a part of it. Consciousness-raising is another part. The day will come when the parts all fit together, and our history and experiences will be different from what they are now. Soon? Maybe. Some of us are working at it.

ARTHUR
April 1971

11

P<small>AUL</small> C<small>LIFFMAN</small>* has a strong body and a strong face and a strong mind. He is intense and shrewd and has been called a "political animal." He is a person that I have loved and resented for a long, long time.

Six years, in fact. We met in December 1964. Paul was working as a film distributor and I was an assistant in the publicity department of a book publishing firm. I had just broken up a stormy relationship with an interior designer from Texas whose middle name was taste. Paul bounced the other way. His middle name was logic.

Paul and I never lived together. At the beginning we saw each other every day. Then six times a week. Then Paul dropped the nine-to-five routine and returned to school to work toward a philosophy doctorate at Columbia, and I went on to bigger and better things as publicity director of children's books for Random House. And we saw each other less.

We did Europe in the fall of 1969. Brussels and Antwerp and Amsterdam and Paris. A week after our return a Little Orphan Annie-haired kid handed us a leaflet on Christopher Street. It told of a meeting of the Gay Liberation Front. At a church, no less. We went.

The congregation consisted of hunky, chunky, big-basketed Village beauties, dressed in radical motley,

* The name Paul Cliffman is fictitious.

spouting movement talk—oppression, consciousness-raising, liberation, pigs—phrases I would hear and use time and time again. The organization was a baby, two or three months old, born out of the gay riots of June 1969, following the raid of the Stonewall bar in Greenwich Village. The Stonewall patrons, many of them young and radical, many transvestites and street people with little to lose, fought back, throwing bricks, breaking windows, ultimately forcing the police to call for reinforcements. From the Stonewall incident stemmed the beginnings of a new movement, the Gay Liberation Front. "Gay is good" became their slogan, gay power a hoped-for reality.

Politics and sex produce electricity. Paul and I needed an electric baby to add current to our relationship. We adopted gay liberation. The baby often proved a bastard.

At the beginning we attended the Gay Liberation Front Sunday night meetings regularly. The early ones were a joy. Characters were defined and established: the gay witch who chaired the meetings, the blond-maned cow-ardly-lion-looking moppet who tore up money at the New York Stock Exchange, the radical lesbian who purred hatred, the six-foot-six transvestite who played basketball before each meeting, and Marty Robinson and Jim Owles.

Marty was a house radical, nervous energy personified, the kid who fascinated me the most. Thin and hollow-cheeked, with short dark hair, black eyes, big feet, and down personality, he was twenty-sevenish, a cat who would fly off the handle at the slightest provocation. He spoke rhetoric, which I didn't understand. Words collided with each other, sort of lower-case nouns without adjectives, the *March of Time* verbalized by Jerry Rubin. His words came out in patches, then quick runs together, with heavy puff-puff breathing; and while the words played a broken melody, the body shifted, not in concert but contradiction, and the eyes darted all over the room, looking everywhere, taking in everything.

Marty hailed from Brooklyn, the son of a well-to-do Jewish family, a carpenter by trade, a thwarted politician, formerly into middle-of-the-road homosexual causes (he was with the staid Mattachine Society), with GLF since its inception. Marty had been using an alias to cover up his movement work. After the Stonewall riot, he dropped the pseudonynm, established an identity, and was in the process of preserving it like sauerkraut juice when I met him.

Marty's counterpoint was Jim Owles, the GLF treasurer, whom I got to know, but never well, during those early days. Jim reminded me of an orphan wandering around a big castle, touching jewels rich in substance, making up names for the treasures, believing in the names, never fully understanding the treasures. He's opinionated, firm to the point of being tight, little-old-mannish. Yet his appearance is pleasant, he's young, he wears his hair young, his clothes young, he's soft-spoken, and fun to be with away from the activist front. Jim had read several books by Ayn Rand and dug her objectivism philosophy: individualism is preferable to collectivism, selfishness to altruism, and nineteenth-century capitalism to any other kind of economic system. Considering his twenty-three years, Jim had a varied background. He took to politics early. The Kennedy campaign started it. While his parents were supporting Nixon, Jim went around distributing pamphlets and petitioning for Kennedy, an act which caused a "political" split between Owles Junior and Senior.

At college Jim took courses in liberal arts with the thought of becoming a history teacher. He had occasional gay experiences, nothing spectacular. When he was eighteen, he joined the Air Force. He claims he was in danger of being drafted and wasn't settled enough in his own mind to check a box divulging his homosexual tendencies. During the two years he served, Jim became involved in anti-war activities concerning GI rights. Stationed in Montana, he circulated petitions and wrote letters to newspapers condemning the draft, the war, and the lack of free speech among GIs. A hassle with his superiors about his anti-war involvement soon brought about a general discharge. He returned to Chicago.

Back home, Chicago was tense and not to his liking. He found the bar scene deadly. In April 1969 he moved to New York.

Soon after the Stonewall incident Jim attended a GLF meeting. He was dressed conservatively, suit and tie. There he met Marty Robinson. Lunar years separated their backgrounds, yet their heads were somewhat in the same place. A June-moon romance developed, based on oppression, ideology, and politics. It satisfied Marty. It partially satisfied Jim, who came to love Marty emotionally as well as logically. Jim's needs, however, weren't being satisfied, and he was silently suffering.

Marty's floor battles and differences in issues with the Gay Liberation Front finally caused him to leave the organization voluntarily. Jim stayed around for one or two weeks after Marty's departure. Meanwhile, Paul Cliffman was pissed off, too, with the weekly character assassinations and havoc that were popular at GLF during that period. On a rainy Sunday afternoon in early November, Paul invited Jim to his apartment to join us for brunch, and to talk about the possibility of forming a new group.

Jim appeared in his Prussian Army jacket, a little annoyed that Paul lived outside of the Village, three subway transfers away. Soon after his coffee Jim relaxed, far more than I had ever seen him, and the discussion got down to the formation of a new group. Jim said that he and Marty had been talking, had in fact mentioned an alternate to GLF to a few of their close acquaintances. One of the basic problems with the Gay Liberation Front, Jim felt, was that GLF aligned itself with all minority groups—Panthers, Cubans, Chicanos, etc. Homosexual needs often were sluffed over for the big picture. For instance, a "crazy" had recently interrupted a Sunday night GLF meeting to report that women were being discriminated against at the Electric Circus. GLF broke up in chaos: half the people left to demonstrate their outrage outside the Circus, the other half stayed to discuss the business at hand.

Why not organize a group based solely on homosexual liberation? Why not have a constitution with a preamble stating goals and purposes? Anything outside of gay liberation would be periphery. We could get involved in the war movement, yes, if we wished to, but on our own. As a group, let's put together a one-issue gay liberation outfit.

Jim suggested a meeting at his apartment the following night. Marty would be there; would Paul and I attend? And so it began.

On November 24, 1969, Paul Cliffman went to an Allen Ginsberg reading at the YMHA Poetry Center —a commitment he couldn't get out of—and I went to the first meeting of the "new group," as we were to call ourselves until we found a name.

In addition to Marty and Jim, there were eight other people present. When I arrived, Marty was deep into a tirade on GLF. We must keep out infiltrators. We must screen our new people. Otherwise GLF could easily send one of their spies to an early meeting and blow the works before we got started.

That over with, we discussed the purpose of the new group. Agreement was reached about drawing up a strong preamble and working from that. It was suggested that we needed to be an activist group, a radical group devoted to the cause of homosexual liberation. The group would take responsible actions only, carefully planned actions working within the framework of our society, actions without violence.

We discussed setting up a community center where gay people could meet for social events as an alternate to the bars and streets. We talked about looking into job discrimination and low-income housing, possibly having an action involving infiltration of a few straight dance bars. (I felt that a big action was needed at the outset to establish the "new group," then a quick follow-up press conference.) We discussed procedures of voting members in and of voting on issues and amendments, and the possibility of having officers each serving a term. And we discussed a twenty-five-cent admission fee per person per meeting.

About names. Gay Activists Movement? Homosexual Activist Movement? Sexual Freedom Front? Gay Action League? None of them seemed right. How about a hit-them-in-the-eye name? Gay Scouts of America? No. Too tricky. We'd think about it and bring back suggestions to the next meeting. Whatever, we would try to incorporate immediately. Jim and Marty would speak to the people at the Oscar Wilde Memorial Book Shop to check with them about legal representation, then we'd somehow borrow two hundred dollars to set up incorporation papers. At midnight we broke up. We were to meet the next Monday, same time, same place. "And think up a good name for the organization. A name that really sings and says something."

The good name didn't come. We settled for a straightforward name, Gay Activists Alliance, initials GAA (gay, get it!). It didn't sing, and it did sound like everything else, but it was better than no name at all. GAA. We'll get used to it.

PAUL AND I were going through a murky period that December. He was on a free and beautiful love (as in screw) everyone kick, and he was loving one guy in particular those nights he wasn't with me, a mustachioed architect in GLF. The weekend of our sixth anniversary—and I tend to be maudlin about such matters—Paul spent with the architect in snowy splendor in upstate New York. I was feeling diseased and unloved, and consequently slept around with a bevy of zeroes, as is my wont. Each sex experience made me lonelier. The idea of free love sounded good in theory, and I would have liked it on a once-a-month basis for me, but I resented it on a big-scale three-times-a-week basis for Paul. A friend during that period—the same Orphan Annie-haired kid who handed us the GLF pamphlet that started it all—said why worry about Paul's sleeping around. He loves you, and the rest is rat cheese. I knew Orphan Annie was right, but I couldn't kick that part of possessiveness that showed its ugly head when I felt I was being neglected. I had mixed feelings, too, about the adulation that Paul received from those moonstruck kids at GLF meetings. The younger kids particularly worshiped him, and Paul was eating up every paw and fawn. He was a strong father sex symbol, with *Goodbye Mr. Chips* overtones. Depending on the amount of sleep I had the night before, I either went along with it or felt like puking.

We held on to our relationship, however weak, Paul seemingly satisfied with status quo, me still hoping. I realize now that the unconscious search during much of my liberation year was for an indefinable outside force—a baby, a French poodle, a business, a cause—that would revitalize our relationship to the beauty peaks it reached during the first couple of years. My new-vitality hope was to get our heads and hearts and bodies together, working on our own baby, our own little Gay Activists Alliance, with Uncle Marty and Uncle Jim, and a militant cast of hundreds to support us along.

On December 21, 1969, at my apartment, the Gay Activists Alliance was officially born. Nineteen people were present to hash out the final version of the GAA preamble and the GAA constitution and to vote for the official officers: the president, vice-president, secretary, treasurer, and delegate at large.

We had previously spent two weeks arguing and discussing the whys and wherefores, the directions and roads of endeavor. Now we had it.

Our preamble, formal and carefully worded (and boy, was each word quibbled over), read as follows:

We as liberated homosexual activists demand the freedom for expression of our dignity and value as human beings through confrontation with and disarmament of all mechanisms which unjustly inhibit us: economic, social, and political. Before the public conscience, we demand an immediate end to all oppression of homosexuals and the immediate unconditional recognition of these basic rights:

The right to our own feelings. This is the right to feel attracted to the beauty of members of our own sex and to embrace those feelings as truly our own, free from any question or challenge whatsoever by any other person, institution, or moral authority.

The right to love. This is the right to express our feelings in action, the right to make love with anyone, any way, any time, provided only that the action is freely chosen by all the persons concerned.

The right to our own bodies. This is the right to treat and express our bodies as we will, to nurture them, to display them, to embellish them, solely in the manner we ourselves determine, independent of any external control whatsoever.

The right to be persons. This is the right freely to express our own individuality under the governance of laws justly made and executed, and to be the bearers of social and political rights which are guaranteed by the Constitution of the United States and the Bill of Rights, enjoined upon all legislative bodies and courts, and grounded in the fact of our common humanity.

To secure these rights, we hereby institute the Gay Activists Alliance, which shall be completely and solely dedicated to their implementation and maintenance, repudiating at the same time violence (except for the right of self-defense) as unworthy of social protest, disdaining all ideologies, whether political or social, and forbearing alliance with any other organization except for those whose concrete actions are likewise so specifically dedicated.

It is, finally, to the imagination of oppressed homosexuals themselves that we commend the consideration of these rights, upon whose actions alone depends all hope for the prospect of their lasting procurement.

Our constitution was an article-by-article, section-by-section breakdown of membership eligibility and selection. ("Every person who has attended at least three meetings within a period of six consecutive meetings is eligible, upon payment of entrance fee.") It listed the duties of the five officers. ("The president is chief executive officer of the organization. He presides at all meetings. He appoints, subject to the approval of the executive committee, all committee chairmen. He assigns projects to appropriate committees. He speaks on behalf of, and in the name of, the organization. He calls all regular and special meetings. He is an ex officio member of all committees. All committee members are responsible to the president for the proper performance of their duties.") It further stated that elections would be held once a year ("candidates to be nominated by the general membership"), and it described the procedures governing a motion of no confidence in an officer.

Additionally, the constitution carried a set of bylaws. Among them: "GAA will not endorse, ally with, or otherwise support any political party, candidate for public office, and/or any organization not directly related to the homosexual cause," and "Meetings shall be conducted according to *Robert's Rules of Order.*"

After voting on the completed version of the constitution, we scribbled down names of people we wanted for various officers. The scraps of paper were dropped into an envelope. Jim Owles won the office of the president and Marty won as delegate at large. Paul and I abstained from being nominated for any of the elected positions since neither of us had the time to do the job well, and we felt we'd do better as representatives from the floor, so to speak.

After the New Year we held our first general meeting at the Church of the Holy Apostles on Ninth Avenue and Twenty-eighth Street. Reverend Weeks, an Episcopal priest, allowed the annex of his church to be used by the Yippies, the Publishers' Media Group, the West Side Discussion Group (a homosexual organization), and the Gay Liberation Front; and now we had a standing commitment for Thursday nights at eight.

The room looked empty. Marty sat at the end of a big folding table looking like a father at dinner while his fifteen children watched for a "go" sign to eat up. One of the men present (only men that evening) questioned the constitution and thought it too tight for a gay organization. He was particularly put off by the section which said a person could be expelled on recommendation of the executive committee. "What an elitist fuck-up," he said, shaking his head and refusing to add his name to the list that was being passed around the room. Our first meeting, and our first minor scuffle. Whee!

Marty reported on our premiere action. We had worked out a petition that we would present to Carol Greitzer, the city councilwoman whose territory included Greenwich Village and areas of the Upper West Side. The trick was to get thousands of signatures to prod Mrs. Greitzer into introducing to the City Council a bill prohibiting public or private employment discrimination on the basis of homosexuality. The petition demanded that, through her office, she work on repealing laws that prohibited participation in homosexual acts between consenting adults. Further, the petition asked that Mrs. Greitzer and her colleagues undertake a campaign to eliminate all discriminatory restrictions to gay businesses.

It was a good starter for a new organization, a chance for us to get out into the streets, meet the public, talk gay "for a cause."

We were hoping to present the signed petitions to Mrs. Greitzer by mid-February, and that would mean a month of heavy campaigning. Mrs. Greitzer, Marty noted, was *not* a champion of homosexual rights. Apparently in 1964 she pushed the police commissioner for plainclothes cops to control "perverts" in Washington Square Park, and in 1966 she was a major force in expanding "Operation New Broom" to the Village area, a campaign that began as a drive to get rid of "undesirables" in the Times Square area.

Marty handed out the blank Greitzer petitions to the potential gay activists. At the same meeting he also mentioned bumping into John Heys, the editor of *Gay Power*. John would run a Gay Activists Alliance column in his biweekly paper if someone would volunteer to write it. I became that volunteer, and at the same time offered to head the publicity committee. (If I could grind out news about Babar the Elephant, why couldn't I moonlight for gay liberation?) Should I keep my own name, bringing disgrace to Random House and my mother and father? Better not. Better change it. So I became Arthur Irving (Irving is my middle name) and two weeks later saw my first Arthur Irving column in print. It began: "There's a new group on the political horizon. It's called Gay Activists Alliance. It's a group you'll be hearing a lot about from now on."

I made a business trip to Chicago for Random House toward the middle of January to wine and dine librarians attending the midwinter conference of the American Library Association. I purposely set up appointments to keep the mornings free in order to attend the Chicago Conspiracy Trial. The effect of those mornings wrecked me. I heard—and still couldn't believe—the decisions of Judge Hoffman, decisions made without justification, decisions made for the sake of preserving the good name of Chicago and its misunderstood mayor. I sat there with my hands tied, watching the embalmment of old America by a dying octogenarian. I sat there watching the killing off of a Woodstock Nation, and I grew nauseated. My head couldn't get back into children's books or librarians, and I remember evenings of automatic niceties while my mind drifted to the horror of the courtroom mornings.

Back home, January 26, to the Village Independent Democrats clubhouse on West Fourth Street. Present are approximately three hundred Village residents, some conservatively dressed, others professionally stylish, Village kickee. On plan, ten members of the new Gay Activists Alliance group mix themselves into this bag. All are gathered to hear campaign speeches of a few well-known New York politicians out campaigning for governorship on the Democratic ticket. Howard Samuels is there, William vanden Heuvel, and Eugene Nickerson. Each candidate makes his speech ever so right and appealing. "I'm against the war." "I'm going to fight Rockefeller." "I'm going to stand up for human rights." Questions follow each speech.

26

The first comes from that clean-shaven young man in the front row, the one who has been applauding so vigorously, who now has his hand up, who surely must be *simpatico.* "My question is what can you do to end the oppression of homosexuals in New York State?" Lo and behold, it's Marty Robinson, and Mr. Samuels is not prepared. It's a question that's never come up in his home town of Oneida, New York, he says, and he's never thought about homosexual oppression enough and really has nothing to say about it. He'll pass.

Eugene Nickerson, though, has something to say. He'll support a law permitting sexual acts between consulting (he means consenting) adults providing a third party isn't hurt. What does he mean—a third party? The audience is confused. Shuffle. Whispers. Now Mr. vanden Heuvel comes to the rescue. A reference to a third party is unnecessary, he says. He will support a law allowing the participation of sexual acts between consenting adults. Period.

Groans and laughs come from the audience surrounding the question-assault team. The homosexual question appears incidental to the important issue of governmental politics. The moderate liberals (Carol Greitzer among them) are anxious to get on to other matters directly concerning them. However disgruntled, or disgusted, the audience does listen, and the following day a contingent of GAA members attends a meeting of the Village Independent Democrats Committee of Human Rights. All of the points in the Carol Greitzer petition are endorsed, and the committee recommends that they set up a meeting with Carol Greitzer and the lovely people of GAA. Score one for the new group.

We were gung-ho in those early days, out to make a name for ourselves. Our next target was the New York *Post*. Columnists Pete Hamill and Harriet Van Horne and Jack Anderson had independently taken swipes at homosexuals, and Marty Robinson thought it time we laid it on the line. He wrote a letter to Mrs. Dorothy Schiff, the *Post*'s publisher, specifically complaining about the Van Horne jibes, demanding a rebuttal, or at least time to make a few "gay is good" points. Mrs. Schiff couldn't afford the time; the *Post* was in the middle of labor negotiations, plus they were moving into a new plant. As a substitute we agreed to an appointment with editor James Wechsler.

Wechsler, a kind roly-poly man, greeted Marty and Paul and me in his top-floor office, apologizing for the disarray and clutter. A week later, he said, he'd be in the new *Post* building, damn, the end of an era. Now he wanted to know about gay liberation, and egged us on about our Van Horne beefs. I got the impression that he didn't particularly care for the lady and wanted an outside hatchet job.

So we explained to Wechsler the need for positive news coverage of homosexuals in establishment newspapers. We talked about the Greitzer petition, constant police harassment, the role of the homosexual in society, his need to feel a sense of pride in himself, and how that pride is dissipated by thoughtless "down" columns. We mentioned the wild possibility of having a homosexual run for political office.

Wechsler's questions were intelligent; he took copious notes, too. He stated that he was responsible only for his own column and claimed that reporter prejudice came partly from a lack of information on homosexual activities. We promised him that that would not be a problem in the future—we'd keep him posted on *all* of our comings and goings.

Subsequently the *Post* was particularly good in its news reportage. They covered most major GAA actions, several minor actions, and did in fact run an editorial on the issue of job discrimination. Ah, the rewards of gay and loud!

I spent a couple of cold February Saturdays getting signatures for the Greitzer petition. Generally, young straight people signed, giving us the right-on flash. In couples, the man would wait for the woman to sign, then sheepishly follow suit. The middle-aged straight white set varied. Some said they would not sign a petition ever; others asked questions about civil rights; still others signed just as a matter of course. Black people almost without exception signed with encouragement. It was with the homosexuals that the problems arose. Generally, the flauntingly gay individual proudly signed, and asked for extra petitions to help us out. But the kid who had a job, the kid who came to the Village once or twice a week to play the bar scene, the kid "passing" for straight, ran to the other side of the street or looked ahead as if the petitioner were invisible, or he became flustered and said, "I'm sorry." Petitioning and leafleting confirmed the fact that many gay people are closeted and terrified of recognition. Most of us found that a day or two of petitioning was educational and good for the soul.

We subsequently formed a street committee to distribute pamphlets and petitions and spread the word about forthcoming GAA actions. The committee would also put out posters and placards for demonstrations, and in effect would be sort of a communications public relations outfit. Marty Robinson headed that committee. In addition to the street and publicity committees, we formed two important functional committees: political action, and a combination pleasure and fund-raising committee. Paul headed political action. Its major function was to recommend new political strategies and to oversee the carrying out of strategies recommended by the membership. Paul's committee met at his apartment once a week to discuss long-range goals and concrete tactics such as lobbying and speaking to special homosexual groups. They also discussed street theater actions, such as a "Gay is proud" invasion of Bloomingdale's to raise political consciousness, letter-writing to city councilmen, and other things.

Our pleasure and fund-raising committee was originally headed by a fine Off Broadway playwright. He, however, left GAA abruptly, and Ron Diamond took over. Ron was a former host at the West Side Discussion Group, tall, loose-limbed, a terrific dancer, a combination love child and astute businessman, the perfect choice for this committee chairmanship. The committee sought to bring funds to GAA through dances and theater parties, rummage sales, auctions, benefits, outings, and other beneficial happy activities. It was a social committee, so it also functioned as an outlet for the kids who weren't ready to come out publicly. They could work behind the scenes at letter-writing, telephone solicitation, hanging crepe paper for a dance. It became one of the most popular committees of GAA, and because of its popularity it ran into trouble in July with the political heads, who got cold feet about the baby movement moving away from their direction.

The publicity committee meetings took place at my apartment the same night that Paul was having the political action committee people at his. I usually had a crew of six to eight eager friends ready to learn the ropes—and work. We made up a cross-indexed file of homosexual organizations, radio and television stations, magazines and newspapers, and columnists, and broke it down so that each of us would be responsible for the feeding of information to one segment of this list. We initiated news releases and discussed future actions to spread the Gay Activists Alliance name.

The organization needed a quick identification symbol. After weeks of designing eagle and cock heads and such, one of our people cleverly came up with the lambda, the eleventh letter of the Greek lower-case alphabet, a sort of upside-down two-pronged check mark. The lambda design is clean, its meaning was right for our group. In chemistry and physics the lambda symbolizes a complete exchange of energy—that moment or span of time that's witness to absolute activity. In a publicity release we noted, "The members of Gay Activists Alliance uphold the lambda as their symbol before the nation. It signifies a commitment among men and women to achieve and defend their human rights as homosexual citizens. Activism is the operative term. Political involvement that is both assertive and effective is GAA's prime thrust. In the struggle against oppression a cultural bond develops, suffused with human energies. The lambda now affirms the liberation of all gay people."

Here is a review of Michelangelo Antonioni's *Zabriskie Point* that I wrote for *Gay Power:*

Antonioni's *Zabriskie Point* is a frightening film and a "must see" for everyone in the movement. I'll go a step further. It's a "must see" for all of us with shaky ideologies, looking for guidance. It's an uncomfortable film, and a brilliant one.

Skipping *Zabriskie* for a moment (I'll weave my way back), and on to politics, I should state that my own politics are the politics of emotion. In political history and concrete and abstract political analysis, I rate a zero. I hear things and see things and react in my own gut way—gut reaction, I guess, being apolitical. The man I love, however, is political. His views are constantly undergoing change, as they should, and presently he is a peaceful activist. He has come to believe, however, that the only way we will see change is by explosive destructive actions aimed at the establishment. (These views are his personal views, and not those of Gay Activists Alliance. Both he and I are with GAA.)

This man—his name is Paul—does not argue politics with me. Sometimes he tells me his thoughts, and I will listen as a student would to a teacher. Last night, for instance, we visited friends in Brooklyn Heights and Paul lucidly explained to them the direction he thought this country would take within the next few years. Now, our friends in Brooklyn are slightly older, professional people, intelligent, not in any movement, television-set activists, and cocktail party demonstrators. And naturally they are fascinated by but uninvolved with our present activities. They were particularly fascinated by Paul's views on revolution, but their "sensible" responses took some of the edge off Paul's "Destroy the evils that bind." Admittedly, I felt myself agreeing with our friends, and silently condemning Paul's political views. That was last night.

Now to today and *Zabriskie Point*. How similar are the thoughts in my head to those played out by the film's girl character, Daria. She reacts the way I react, thinks the way I think, does what I think I would do. She's discontented. She's halfheartedly running away from establishment and the smell of status quo—a smell that she doesn't find totally distasteful. But Daria, unfortunately, doesn't know what she's running to. She rides her car through the desert, listening to music on the radio, more comforting, she says, than news reports. She meets a young man. He may have just shot and killed a cop in a campus riot (the same cop who had shot and killed an unarmed Black student). The young man has stolen a plane to escape, and has flown it to the desert. Here, at Zabriskie Point, the two take off to an arid wasteland, and groove and groove and groove. They return to the plane, paint it with symbols of love. He then flies the plane to Phoenix to return it. Police cars surround the vehicle when it lands, and shoot him dead—tat for tit for tat.

The picture is fascinating and the ending brilliant. Daria returns to her employer, a successful real estate promoter. Bereaved by her lover's death, disgusted with the symbols of a dead society that led to his death and that now surround her, Daria imagines the total destruction of America. The destruction on film comes first in a series of fires, then in brilliant explosions, the slow-motion camera picking up fragments of books, of food, of plastic man. This tableau ending has to be the most terrifying in the history of film.

I saw *Zabriskie Point* at a screening with a *Hello Dolly*

type audience. There was shuffling during the film, and bad word-of-mouth after the film. The discontent had nothing to do with the film's direction or acting. It had everything to do with the shocking subject matter. Face it, I thought, America is destroying itself, but wants to be entertained.

Perhaps the shock value of *Zabriskie Point* to me was the shock that the "Pauls" could be destroyed by America at the same time that they are acting out its destruction. Perhaps it was the corruptness of the plastic society, the helmeted cops, the smog-filled sky of Phoenix, juxtaposed with the uncertain principles of the girl and the certain principles of the boy, ultimately destroyed, that put me into this mood that I'm in. Certainly the corruption of America, personified in *Zabriskie* time and again, is the corruption that, among other things, has led to the suppression of the homosexual in America. Antonioni—and Paul—may be right. We may all go down in slow-motion takes. *Zabriskie* makes the distinct possibility of total annihilation real, and it makes me shudder.

O<small>N</small> M<small>ARCH</small> 5 we threw our first big action—at City Hall, no less—and with press coverage. We had enough members (nearly forty) to plan a full-scale protest to demand that Mayor John Lindsay take action to end police harassment and job discrimination against homosexuals in New York. We planned the picket line for nine A.M., a totally unreasonable hour for man, beast, and gay activist—even those of us with daytime jobs.

Nevertheless, out of the subways we tumbled, in twos and threes, in beards and peacoats, with Mennen-shaved skin, with sleep in our eyes, and posters under our arms. The photographers and reporters were there to greet us. They followed us from the subway to City Hall, taking outrageous shots, asking outrageous questions. "What does that sign mean—'The Gay Voting Block Swung the Mayoral Election'? What Gay Voting Block?" We told them.

The cops were out in platoons. Somehow, word leaked beforehand. They tried to stop us from entering City Hall. Others were entering, why couldn't we? They told us that we were a group, only private citizens could enter. Keep back, get out, they warned, astride their horses, stout-hearted bluecoats with shiny nightsticks, guarding the bastion from homosexuals.

Despite warnings, Jim Owles tried to get in. They evicted him bodily, then put up the police barricades.

They blocked off the City Hall promenade, and a mini minor city official stood behind the barricade line and offered us a midi minor city official as a Lindsay substitute. We didn't want him. We wanted the mayor. No dice, we were told. Lindsay's in Buffalo. You can not enter City Hall.

We formed a picket line, Paul acting as marshal, professionally angry, eating up every minute of it. When we were not talking to the press, we held our signs high and proud. "Gay Is Proud." "Gay Is Good." "Equality for Homosexuals." We were a beautiful bunch that day, rising up gay, Marty and Paul and Jim and Ron Diamond and Ralph Hall (a fellow reporter from *Gay Power*) and the lovely people from the publicity committee getting their first real taste of community and liberation.

Noon came, and the working class spilled out of their office jobs to their Woolworth lunches. Men with attaché cases, Wall Street clerks and secretaries. "What kind of protest is that?" "Homosexuals, ha, ha, ha. What do they want?"

But they dug it. They dug the long-haired guitar player improvising songs about love, sodomy, law, Lindsay, and the little piggies that protect City Hall. How they dug it! "This is the best protest I've ever seen, and I've been coming to them for years," said a Chase Manhattanite on the run.

The press felt our vibes, too. Cameras ground as men kissed men, establishment cameras carefully avoiding the phallic symbol embroidered on Ralph Hall's sweater. And questions. So many questions. "How do the sodomy laws suppress homosexuals?" "Do your parents know?" "How would it feel if your parents knew?" "Are you proud of what you're doing?" "Ashamed?" And ever so timidly, "What do you guys do in bed?"

The sight that they saw and the answers they got quickly negated any concept of namby-pamby homosexuality. Here, for all Wall Street, City Hall, and the press of America, were honest-to-God flesh-and-blood gorgeous, gorgeous gays. Stereotypes? Gone with the wind.

Eventually an emissary arrived from City Hall. Michael Dontzin, the mayor's counsel and adviser. He'd see three of us—Jim Owles, the *Gay Power* photographer, and me with my tape recorder. We were taken into an austere office. Curved windows, Japanese dolls in glass cases, bad oil paintings of heroes of yesteryear—James Monroe, 1758–1831—American flags, upholstered chairs with U.S. eagles embroidered in navy blue. Michael Dontzin entered. "I want no pictures taken" were his first words. Then, "My own feeling is that I'm more interested in dealing with the substance of the matter than in getting involved in any public relations or press dealings. I'm the mayor's counsel and one of his close advisers and part of his inner-policy committee, and since he is out of town, they've asked me to come, since they thought you should see somebody who has some standing in the administration."

Dontzin, a short man with a look of having just emerged from a barber's chair via a haberdasher's shop, discussed the problems of homosexuality in New York with Jim, specifically police harassment of public subway toilets, harassment of homosexual steam baths, and the general prejudicial badgering of homosexually-owned businesses particularly the non-Mafia-run gay bars. Jim mentioned the Carol Greitzer petition and talked about the fair

37

employment law and about our organizational campaign to repeal the sodomy and solicitation laws. Jim noted that the mayor had never come out with a positive statement about homosexual rights, and he stressed that Lindsay and other political figures must listen to our gripes, talk to us in public forums, help us when help was needed. A line of communication had to be opened between the gay community and the mayor's office. Homosexuals were responsible for a good many votes in New York, Jim continued, and it was time the mayor's office recognized this fact.

Dontzin listened intently. Occasionally he would comment. He said he believed that police had let up on entrapment and that they had stopped hiding behind screens in public toilets. In some city areas, he said, the officers are rougher than in others. There is nothing that can be done about a uniformed man's innate prejudices. Lindsay, he said, is sensitive to the problems of the city's homosexuals. And "he has no preconceived notions or prejudices about anybody, including people whose sexual outlets are different in the 'normal' sense."

Dontzin said he'd present our demands to the mayor upon Lindsay's return from Buffalo. He bade us a warm farewell—told us he would get back to us shortly, that his door was always open, but call for an appointment first.

Outside, the anxious crew ran up to Jim to find out what happened. I was taken aback to hear Jim report, "Just some more cover-up garbage from a lackey." This didn't seem to me to be the case, and I questioned Jim about his statement privately. He shrugged his shoulders and said, "What else could I say?"

Later that day Lindsay's press assistant released a statement: Michael Dontzin, the mayor's counsel, considered the Gay Activists Alliance's grievances properly presented and perfectly valid, and will pursue them and report diectly to the mayor.

That evening we watched ourselves on ABC-TV news, gloating at the sight of our own happy faces, proud that our march on City Hall was successful, and ready and eager for another full-scale attack on the forces that oppressed us.

That attack, sure enough, took place three days later as a result of a freaky mistimed raid on an after-hours drinking spa, the Snake Pit.

Paul and I woke up early that Snake Pit morning, my head still buzzing from a loud adventure with the Theater of the Ridiculous the night before. Agonizingly I shuffled to the bathroom, pumped myself with aspirins, turned on the faucet and the radio, and got the news, courtesy WCBS: Two hundred arrested in raid of after-hours bar in Greenwich Village. One unidentified man seriously hurt, taken to St. Vincent's Hospital.

I did not have to add two and two to get four. I signaled the news to Paul, pulled myself together, and started phoning.

WCBS could tell me no more than that which had been reported. The officer in charge of the Sixth Precinct could tell me nothing. Someone in the public relations office at St. Vincent's Hospital said that a person had either jumped or fallen from a second-floor window of the Charles Street police station. He had been impaled on a spiked picket fence. Portions of the fence had to be sawed away and taken along with the man to the hospital. The patient was presently in surgery. The surgeons were working with a rescue crew using special saws to cut away portions of the spike. The man's name—Diego Vinales. His condition—critical.

Further calls revealed that the raid took place at five A.M. at a tiny dark basement den on West Tenth Street, aptly called the Snake Pit. One hundred and sixty-seven people arrested for disorderly conduct, held for three or four hours, served with summonses, and released. Four charged with violating liquor laws. Diego Vinales charged with attempting to escape arrest. The Snake Pit charged with creating a hazardous or physically offensive condition by an act which serves no legitimate purpose (specifically serving alcohol after hours).

Paul and I canceled our Sunday afternoon bicycle excursion. I called Jim and Marty. No answer. Called again. No answer. Then I got on the phone with Bob Kohler, a Gay Liberation Front leader, and suggested to him that the entire homosexual community of New York hold a mass protest action that evening. Bob thought it couldn't be done on such short notice. I got on the phone to Jim and Marty again and finally got them. They had heard the news. I suggested that we call our complete membership to an emergency meeting. Two hours later thirty members appeared at their apartment, plus a guest star, a fellow that we all knew from Gay Liberation Front. He had been arrested at the Snake Pit. The fellow recollected the incidents of the early morning. It was pure nightmare.

An act of indignation had to be made that very day. We opted for a mass protest march and a vigil at St. Vincent's Hospital for Diego Vinales.

Then we went to work. We wrote up a pamphlet: "Any way you look at it, Diego Vinales was pushed. We are all being pushed. A march on the Sixth Precinct will take place tonight, March 8, at 9 P.M., gathering at Sheridan Square. Anyone who calls himself a human being, who has the guts to stand up to this horror, join us. A silent vigil will occur immediately following the demonstration."

Marty Robinson used his ingenuity to find a mimeo machine in a locked-up city on a cold winter Sunday. Eventually he was able to run off a fair number of pamphlets. They were distributed to groups of two, and the groups took to Central Park West, the Upper East Side, and the Village. Meanwhile, I was on the phone to news media, talking to most of the same people I had spoken to four days previously for the City Hall zap. There were a couple of encouraging signs of recognition: "Oh, yes, GAA, we'll come." That done with, Paul and I pamphleted the West Village bars. Word had already spread to many of the Sunday afternoon beer drinkers. We were given an open-door reception in gin mills that ordinarily would be up tight about in-house pamphleting. Bartenders in two of the tackier establishments took additional circulars to distribute to their later turnover of customers.

Word about the demonstration spread like wildfire. About five P.M. there was also a rumor that Diego Vinales had died. The rumor started with a false FM newscast and was picked up by the huskies at the Stud. By the time Paul and I had run out of pamphlets and were in the process of returning to Jim and Marty's apartment, people stopped us on the street to say that the gay movement had its first martyr in Diego Vinales.

At their apartment I called St. Vincent's. Vinales, they said, was alive, but fighting for his life.

Marty, meanwhile, was like a tiger on the prowl, pacing

back and forth, excited and jumpy. He informed us that the Gay Liberation Front had gotten in touch with a number of movement groups to participate in the demonstration. A huge turnout was expected.

I left for Sheridan Square with Marty to clue in the press on what was happening. A *New York Times* reporter was there, a couple of raincoats from the *Daily News*, a photographer from the New York *Post*, John Heys of *Gay Power*, several independent cameramen, but no visible television cameras. GAA friends soon appeared on the scene, and shortly thereafter we were joined by the Gay Liberation Front people, Women's Liberation, the Yippies, Homosexuals Intransigent, the Homophile Youth Movement, and many, many members of the gay community who were not affiliated with organizations, including several faces that I recognized from the afternoon pamphleting. Perhaps four hundred people in all.

We began our march to the Charles Street police station. The chants rang out: "Say it loud, gay is proud," "Gay power to the gay, gay people." At the station, police barricades, old hat by this time, were spread out blocking the street entranceway. The riot squad was visible near the precinct house. Tactical Patrol Force, regular cops, the whole militia. A yell rang out for the police captain, Salmeiri. He refused to appear. The chants continued. "Who gets the payoff? The police get the payoff!" Amid the turmoil Jim Owles spoke to an officer in charge of the defensive line. Three homosexual representatives should be allowed to enter the station and verbally confront Captain Salmeiri on the Snake Pit raid, said Jim. It was imperative—the air was charged with riot potential. Getting a statement from Salmeiri might mollify the crowd. No dice, said the officer in charge. And so the chants continued for Salmeiri's blood.

Meanwhile, a physical wreck standing next to me shouted, "They're yelling for the wrong person."

"Who's the right person?" I yelled back.

"Inspector Pine."

"Who's Inspector Pine? And how do you know he's the right person?"

"Pine is responsible for the Stonewall raid and for last night's raid on the Pit. I know, because I'm the lover of Schatzy, the owner of the Snake Pit. And I was at the door last night when it happened."

The man, whoever he was, looked as if he hadn't slept for three days. He was wearing big black sunglasses, and his face was pinched, and I was close enough to smell his breath. It was bad. He was probably about twenty-eight or twenty-nine, maybe a few years younger, the kind of face that doesn't see daylight often, and night too often. I asked him if I could take him for a drink and told him I'd probably write up the Snake Pit story for *Gay Power*. Would he give me an inside view of last night's events? "Yes, but keep my name out of it." I promised I would.

We toddled behind the marchers until we reached St. Vincent's Hospital. He had been at St. Vincent's several times that day to check on Vinales' condition. It was still critical. "There's nothing to do but wait," he said. "Let's get that drink."

At the Finale we each had a couple of bourbons, straight. We ordered fried chicken. He couldn't eat his, and ordered another drink. I asked if he'd mind talking about the raid. I placed my tape recorder on the table between us. Here's his story:

43

I was at the door, about five A.M., at the Snake Pit, with my lover, Schatzy, when the raid took place. The Pit is not Mafia controlled. It's what we call in our profession a legally run place, but it's open after hours. It's run by Schatzy alone, and he takes care of everybody. He's known by everybody in the Village. He's beautiful people. But to operate in the Village you have to pay off. I can tell you down to the last penny what Schatzy pays and I can tell you who he pays, but I'm not authorized to say that.

Tonight everybody was out yelling for the captain of the Sixth Precinct. He had little to do with the raid. We pay these people off, but when someone bigger steps in, then the smaller cops have to do something.

Deputy Inspector Seymour Pine of the First Division is the guy behind the raids. Pine is looking for a reputation. He wants to be chief inspector. Pine said last night that he was going to close the Village up. The precinct is riled up about gays.

About five A.M. a guy showed up at the door of the Pit with a warrant. He said, "Can I talk to you for a minute?" Schatzy stepped outside the door. They pushed him back and forced their way in.

Then they took us away. Nobody told us about our rights or why we were being arrested. Nobody was told a word. I tried to ask a cop when they were arresting us, "What rights do we have?" and the cop said, "Shut your fucking mouth."

We were treated like animals at the station. We were all herded into one big room. There was a shoeshine machine there. A couple of the kids turned on the machine and started shining their shoes and the cops started coming over and getting mad. One cop came and called me a faggot. He said, "You're nothing but a prick," and said, "I'm going to tear off both of your fucking feet if you don't get off that machine."

If the Snake Pit was a straight bar, everyone would have been let go. If it was a straight after-hours bar, they would have taken in the people who ran the place. But this guy Pine wants to make it really big, so he takes all these people in, gives them a summons and tells them when he gives them a summons you don't have to show if you don't want to. Nobody pays bail. But the idea is to drag everybody down there and make a big scene about illegally running a bar after hours. After the Stonewall riot last summer they tried to cool it down for a while, but they're starting up again. The cops took all the money from Schatzy's cash register, and the kids' tips. They didn't return any of it. About four hundred dollars.

The cops had no legal right to enter the way they entered. They had no legal right to drag all those people down and give them a summons then tell them they didn't have to show up. Let's face it. If those people who were arrested really got up tight about it, they could turn around and sue whoever they wanted to sue because of false arrest. They can't prove disorderly conduct, they can't even prove that those people were there. The people who were arrested weren't checked for identification or pills or anything. It was a sick, illegal thing.

Diego Vinales was frightened stiff. My own opinion is that he didn't know what was happening. He'd never been in anything like this before. He was afraid maybe he'd be put in jail or something like that. Diego ran up the stairs and tried to jump from the window to the other ledge and didn't make it.

I was at the window right after he landed on the spikes.

45

The remarks the cops made after this happened were unbelievable. One cop said to a fireman, "You don't have to hurry, he's dead, and if he's not, he's not going to live long." I was with three or four kids when one of the kids heard this who happened to be a friend of Diego's. He started crying and screaming out. Then the other kids started crying. They saw what was happening and they were shaken. But the remarks kept coming from the cops. They probably thought they were justified. Diego was a faggot, they said. They used the word faggot so many times it was unbelievable.

Diego had a friend whom he came in with last night. I had never seen him before but he was sort of an average guy, from what I could make out talking to him. Diego was good-looking, about twenty-five, had a beautiful body. He lived in Jersey, and said he came from Argentina.

We'll probably have a martyr in Diego if he doesn't pull through this, and it hurts me that we may have one. I feel so sorry that this happened. It may be good for the cause, but no man's life is worth any amount of money or sacrifice. A man's life is sacred.

At the police station one of the straight cops just shook his head. He said, "I'm sorry. I'm just plain sorry."

My own head hurts. I still hear Diego crying out in pain and I hear him moaning and screaming. It isn't easy to shake.

I put Schatzy's lover in a cab and headed back toward Jim and Marty's apartment. The place was packed. Apparently, after I split from the march, the demonstrators left St. Vincent's and headed back to Sheridan Square. Marty and Jim did a wind-up spiel thanking their brothers for participating. This antagonized their sisters who weren't thanked, especially the Women's Lib contingent. A few of the more vocal sisters loudly accused GAA of elitism and male chauvinism.

But the mood at the apartment was "We did it again," and the lack of tact at Sheridan Square and the horror of the Snake Pit were momentarily forgotten. GAA had another victory to celebrate. Tomorrow, the world.

The following day Marty Robinson delivered an impassioned indictment at the Village Independent Democrats Club of society's treatment of the homosexual. The club passed a resolution calling for a moratorium on raids of all bars frequented by homosexuals. Bob Egan, the president of the club, wrote a letter to Mayor Lindsay stating, "We request this moratorium in order to be free, along with other community groups, to study the facts of the Snake Pit incident together with the overall conduct of the police and the State Liquor Authority and to determine whether or not there was a concerted effort under way to harass homosexuals in the Village community."

My interview with Schatzy's lover appeared as a front page story in *Gay Power*. Shortly thereafter editor John Heys received a telephone call from Inspector Pine explaining his reasons for raiding the Snake Pit—he was just doing his job. Several days later *The New York Times* ran a column stating that Democratic-Liberal Representative Edward Koch accused New York City Police Commissioner Howard Leary of permitting the Police Department to resume a policy of harassing homosexuals with illegal arrests. The *Times* also quoted an executive assistant district attorney as saying that virtually all of the charges of

47

disorderly conduct at the Snake Pit were dismissed in court because "the police could not make a legal case."

(Ten months later seven of the 167 "made a legal case" against the city by testifying in hearings before the examiner of the Corporation Counsel of the City of New York. Each sued the city for false arrest and false imprisonment to the tune of $75,000, or a grand total of $525,000. The seven claimed they were threatened, subjected to verbal abuse, and not informed of their rights or of the charges pressed against them. The case, as of this date, is still pending.)

Four or five weeks later Inspector Pine was transferred from his power post at the First Precinct to the Sixty-second Precinct in the Flatbush area of Brooklyn. GAA immediately ground out a pamphlet for street distribution: "A tree may grow in Brooklyn, but this Pine will wither away."

Meanwhile, news from St. Vincent's was that Diego Vinales was off the critical list. Since he was still technically under arrest and not allowed visitors, I sneaked into the hospital the last week of March with the hope of getting an interview with Diego for *Gay Power*. He was in a semiprivate ward on the fourth floor. Outside his room the television blared, "Manischewitz wishes you a happy Passover," while eight men in wheelchairs rocked back and forth, their identification tags jiggling on their wrists. There was a feeling of conviviality in the hallway, even among the two policemen who didn't see me pass by. They, too, were watching television.

Diego Vinales was startled to see a stranger in a trench coat. Apparently I was his first visitor outside of the friend who had accompanied him to the Snake Pit that eventful night. Vinales seemed to want to talk, his voice was weak, and I had to sit close to the bed in order to hear him speak.

He was handsome, all right. Dark hair, shiny eyes, tight skin of a copperish yellow tone. He had three bandages on his body above his waist. His head was propped up with a pillow and he was heavily tranquilized, yet worried about an operation which was due the next day.

But more than the operation, he was worried about his chances of staying in America. He admitted he was in the country illegally—his visa had expired—and he was terrified when the police invaded the Snake Pit, terrified enough to attempt escape, terrified enough to jump from a second-story window.

He said he wanted to get well, to return to his job and live a quiet life. He suspected that his parents in Argentina might have heard about the Snake Pit incident. He hadn't written to them, but he had relatives in the States who might have picked up the news and transmitted it to his family.

He said that his visit to the Snake Pit was his first to a gay bar in New York. He had been to the Village only once before, to take in the local sights. He did not talk much about the raid, or about the scars and wounds he'll be carrying with him for the rest of his life. He was grateful for the support from the various gay groups. He asked that I call him by his nickname, Tito, and made me promise to come back again as soon as he recovered from his next operation. I promised him I would, and I did.

GAA WORKED well for Paul and me during those months when the group concentrated its activities on outside actions as opposed to internal politics. I was developing a surer sense of myself as a result of writing the *Gay Power* columns, and, of course, that strength helped our relationship considerably. Paul began to emerge from his long-standing academic cocoon during that period. His homosexual liberation activities were becoming as important as his dissertation on Dionysius the Pseudo-Areopagite—and just when I finally learned to pronounce the man's name.

Paul was delighted, too, with the publicity committee's planned action to infiltrate the Easter Parade, even though Marty Robinson and Jim Owles thought it gauche, if not silly. The committee decided to meet at noon on Easter Sunday at the fountain in front of the Plaza Hotel. Dress optional: suits or khakis or calicoes or jeans. Then we'd join the strollers in a display of homosexual affection for the benefit of photographers and television cameras, as well as for our own sheer enjoyment. Unfortunately it snowed. Torrents. Our Easter Parade action was called off.

Easter Sunday evening my parents called. They were snowbound in New York, on their way to Montreal from Florida. I joined them for dinner. As usual, they asked what I was up to. I took a deep breath and told them.

Although both have known for years about my homo-sexuality, it was a subject that was seldom if ever talked about. The fact that I was now politically involved and working for a "good cause" pleased them. My father said he had read about Vinales' impalement in the *Daily News,* and he was curious to know the inside story. My mother seemed concerned about my welfare—she didn't want me bumped off by the Mafia or the police department—and asked that I send her the *Gay Power* columns as they appeared. Both asked if Paul Cliffman was responsible for my political involvement. To that I answered yes and no.

Since that Easter Sunday revelation, my relationship with my parents has improved. I no longer send them weather reports, but write about activities, if not feelings, and consequently receive newspaper clippings from Montreal about "liberation" as reported by the Canadian press. I'm still not sure if they're aware of what gay liberation is about, but in the words of my friend Holly Woodlawn, "It's nice."

On Monday, April 13, the Metropolitan Museum of Art celebrated its one hundredth anniversary. Mayor John Lindsay was scheduled to meet and greet the first hundred guests and to address himself to the general public from the steps of the newly renovated museum. We were there.

We arrived early to be included among the first hundred in line. Discriminately, we spread ourselves among the mere mortals who weren't gay activists, and we clutched the pamphlets we would soon distribute: "Mr. Mayor, we are now initiating into City Council a bill prohibiting job discrimination on the basis of sexual preference. We again ask you to speak out in support of the principles of this proposed legislation. Last month, we went to City Hall. At that time, your counsel, Michael Dontzin, promised to bring this matter to your attention. WHY HAVEN'T YOU RESPONDED?"

The weather was perfect. At 9:55 A.M. Mayor Lindsay strode up the museum's front steps. He was greeted by director Thomas Hoving. A band swung into "The Star-Spangled Banner," and Mr. Hoving introduced "our landlord."

The mayor grinned his little-boy grin. He thanked the museum patrons "who care deeply enough about the city and art to recognize their mutual dependency." He noted that the museum and the city had "nourished each other for one hundred years" and extolled the new plaza for "extending the museum's beauty out into the street."

By paying too much mind to the celebrities and the band and the high school kids and the museum patrons and the milling throng of out-of-towners, the police paid no mind at all to the young man who was slowly ascending the museum steps to the podium where Lindsay was perched.

"When are you going to speak out on homosexual rights, Mr. Mayor?" came like a bolt of lightning out of Marty Robinson's mouth. The contrast of Marty in his basketball jacket next to Lindsay in his navy blue suit was a picture no artist could paint. Police immediately surrounded Marty, pulling him out of sight.

Soon after, the mayor strolled around the new water fountain, smiling constantly while the water spurted in leaps and bounds, courtesy of a master control switch operated by a master controller in a secret room somewhere in the museum. I followed a few steps behind Lindsay, and climbed the steps with him as he entered the museum. One of our people gave him a pamphlet, and I watched Jim Owles step alongside him and heard Jim say, "You have our leaflet. Now when the hell are you going to speak to homosexuals?" The mayor smiled.

He kept his smile as our members individually shook his hand and asked him questions about homosexual rights. Some held the mayor's grip so long that police had to pull them away. As Lindsay proceeded on a brief tour of the museum, Paul and a Columbia crony named Morty Manford linked arms and shouted, "Gay power, gay power," in the foyer of the museum. It hit a sour note for me. I was having bad feelings about what GAA was doing for the first time.

I've always admired Lindsay. I feel he's an honest man doing a mediocre job in the crooked game of politics. His integrity is often responsible for his failings. It may be a romantic notion, but Lindsay and the Metropolitan Museum exemplify a part of New York that's somewhat sacred to me, and to see them both under attack, no matter how valid the attack, was disturbing. I made a couple of ugly remarks to Paul and Morty and whoever else was around to hear me, and returned to Random House in an ugly mood. I did little but curse my typewriter the rest of the working day.

I felt far less critical of our Lindsay attack at a television taping six days after the Metropolitan zap.

With Mayor Lindsay is a half-hour program shown in

53

the New York area Sunday evenings at 10:30. The program is usually taped three hours in advance at the WNEW studios on East Sixty-seventh Street.

Not long after the City Hall demonstration, the membership discussed a secret indoor non-escape direct attack on the Mayor at WNEW. We set the date for April 19, and each of us was to write for tickets in order to thoroughly infiltrate the studio.

By the middle of April we had collected forty tickets. There was no public statement by the mayor, of course, and his silence gave us a legitimate reason to go ahead with the zap.

At four P.M. that Sunday forty people met at my apartment, a walking distance to the TV station. Paul's political action committee prepared a number of questions to ask Lindsay, and at the rehearsal meeting Paul coached us on when and how to chant, when to applaud, when to stamp our feet, ways and means of making the most of a situation in which the mayor might conceivably loosen up—or we might conceivably find ourselves in jail on a public nuisance charge.

Close to six P.M. we filed out of the apartment in small groups and headed toward WNEW. Many GAA people were already in line when I arrived. I asked an usher to direct me to the studio where the Lindsay show would be shot, walked in, and sat myself down next to the producer, who asked me to leave. The gall.

On my way back to the end of the line I spotted Michael Dontzin. "Hello," he said. "I see you have some of your people here."

"Why haven't we heard from you?" I asked.

"I didn't know I was to get back to you. Let's get together next week and talk."

I told Dontzin I had called his office several times since our City Hall demonstration six weeks ago and had left messages galore with his secretary. He apologized, said he was over his head with work, and insisted that Jim and I try again. He'd notify his secretary to set up an appointment for the following week. He queried me again about the GAA turnout for that particular show—a show on ecology with Arthur Godfrey. I played dumb and walked him back to the studio from which I had just been evicted. I took a front row seat.

By then Lindsay was very much present. He wore a dark blue suit, a light blue shirt, a red tie, an ecology button, and he looked fabulous but nervous. His hands were firmly tucked into his pants pockets, and he crossed and uncrossed his legs several times, to the right, to the left, to the right, to the left.

As the studio audience filed in, Lindsay's eyes absorbed them one by one. Lord knows what he was thinking. One-third of the house was "us."

The program begins. A canned musical introduction: Leonard Bernstein's "Something's Coming." Show credits. Commercials. Then Arthur Godfrey, introduced as "the nation's number one advocate of ecology and preservation." Godfrey takes a seat next to the mayor, and Lindsay, with his hands in his pockets, reads from the teleprompter, "Tomorrow night is the first night of Passover. I'd like to wish all of our neighbors a good week." The audience watches in silence. Lindsay's hands come out of his pockets and twiddle, his legs uncross. "Our city workers earn

55

their money, they do a good job," he says. His eyes are the same color blue as his shirt.

Godfrey speaks. "Soot is what the housewife sees the most of," he says, and suddenly ZAP.

Paul Cliffman lunges out. "Mr. Mayor, what are you doing to end job discrimination against homosexuals?" The mayor tugs his ear, Arthur Godfrey fidgets like mad, and a loud eruption takes place in the audience. A stampede of stamping feet. Voices everywhere: "Answer the question, answer the question." Someone yells, "Are you in favor of repeal of the sodomy laws?" The TV cameras stop rolling. Paul is pulled out of sight by a security guard. And the mayor quietly says "My counsel Michael Dontzin will meet with those who want to see him outside." Then someone from the mayor's staff announces, "You cannot disrupt a public meeting under threat of arrest. You either leave in peace or are under arrest." Nobody pays him mind.

Lindsay and Godfrey, meanwhile, are looking terribly uncomfortable. A nervous smile brightens the mayor's face but soon disappears. A cameraman says, "Let's pick it up from . . ." In back of me a straight member of the audience says, "Lindsay has to read off tapes. He can't answer questions unless he has prepared answers. Now he's threatening arrest." The program continues. Godfrey rambles on. "People cause the pollution," he says. "People have an indifferent attitude about pollution." And again the interruptions come. Interruptions that soon take the form of a ritual. Godfrey or Lindsay makes a statement on ecology, the statement is picked up by a Gay Activists Alliance person and thrown back at Lindsay in gay terms. Godfrey talks about abandoned junk cars. Phil Raia, one of our new members, shouts, "And what about abandoned homosexuals?" The cameras stop. Phil is led from the audience. Lindsay suggests that one-way bottles—nonreturnable—might help in the elimination of pollution. Jim Owles shouts, "What about a one-way mayor—nonreturnable?" He makes a finger sign as he's led from the studio. On noise pollution the mayor says, "If you're stuck in a traffic jam, it's illegal to blow your horn," and another member comments, "It's illegal in New York to blow anything," and leaves the studio to much stamping and applauding. The looks on the faces of Godfrey, Lindsay, and the program director read, "What next?"

As expected, none of the disruptions are shown on the videotape that evening. A word or two, or some applause in the background, but the finished show is clean and antiseptic—and dull.

After the program I talked to Dontzin again. Like an exasperated father he scolded us for being bad boys and girls and set up a definite appointment for April 29 with "three or four of your people so you can talk to Deputy Mayor Richard Aurelio."

The three or four turned out to be Marty Robinson, Jim Owles, Paul, the news correspondent for a rival paper called *Gay*, and me.

We were ushered into the Michael Dontzin Early American room at City Hall by a mini-skirted beauty who told us that Mr. Dontzin and Aurelio, along with Harry Taylor, the chief of patrol, would join us in a minute. Taylor was acting as representative for Police Commissioner Leary.

My first impression of Aurelio was that he bore a strong resemblance to the late Ernie Kovacs, complete with cigar, thick glasses, and a stick of hair falling down his forehead. From the onset Aurelio let it be known that he didn't like our public confrontations with the mayor and hoped that they would stop. I replied that the confrontations would not be necessary if Lindsay would speak out publicly on gay issues. Then Marty produced a notebook with a list of demands that he had prepared for the occasion. First a moratorium on police raids and harassment to give time to the authorities "to work on solutions to the underlying problems of the State Liquor Authority and Police Department corruption." Chief Taylor winced. I chimed in, "Since the raids on the Stonewall and the Snake Pit and the resulting riots, homosexuals will no longer sit back and take shit from the police. One of the reasons we're here is to forewarn you that spontaneous riots might break out again this summer if police harassment continues." At that point Taylor broke in with the happy news that Inspector Pine of Snake Pit fame had been transferred to Brooklyn. And Aurelio noted, "It's not the policy of the Police Department to harass homosexuals per se."

Paul interjected that homosexuals experience two types of harassment: one that goes under the color of law (that is, with legal justification to some degree) and the other under the color of no law (with no legal justification, and with charges dismissed because they do not hold up legally). "This last type of harassment must stop immediately," Paul said. "We will not tolerate it. Often police direct verbal abuses at homosexuals that are disgusting. We demand that a directive go out that this police practice stop."

Taylor replied that harassment was in no way an implied policy in police quarters and that harassment of homosexuals came only in isolated instances. "In some cases we get letters of complaint about an establishment by residents of the area. Sometimes they complain of too much noise, and we follow through by serving summonses, but only when it is necessary to do so."

Jim turned to Aurelio. "There's a moral issue and a political issue at stake here. Lindsay owes a political debt to his homosexual constituents. He owes us his support both politically and humanistically. Yet we don't exist as far as the New York public is concerned. We demand public recognition by the mayor. It's absolutely essential."

Marty then submitted his list of demands to Aurelio. Taylor, insisting that he understood our situation, said he would set up a series of meetings between GAA and high-ranking police officers of various city precincts. He claimed that Commissioner Leary stated a willingness to meet with us and would do so at a later date if we deemed it necessary.

During all this, a game was being played, with Aurelio and Dontzin on one team, Taylor on the other. It was as if the Police Department was working independently of the mayor's office. There was an underlying antagonism to the points of view presented by the two teams that had nothing at all to do with the homosexual rights issue. A feeling of hostility permeated the room. The teams were showing off to each other—and to us. I doubted the sincerity of Taylor and Dontzin and Aurelio about the summer moratorium, and my doubts were to be well founded. At the end of August a new rash of police harassment broke out on Forty-second Street. And we had our end-of-summer riot, as prophesied.

Meanwhile, we were close to Carol Greitzer petition

presentation time. Originally we had planned to visit her at the end of February, but we hadn't enough signatures. The weather was bad, and we were procrastinating.

In late March Ray Rivera joined GAA. Ray was unlike any other member. He was a street transvestite. He was earnest and open. He was gay and proud and loud, and he got busted on Forty-second Street for petitioning.

He told us about the bust at one of our Thursday night meetings. I thought it might be terrific to make a mountainous issue of his arrest and to support him throughout his trial appearances. Ray was willing to go all the way to embarrass the pig authorities for his injustice. He had had a sniff of gay liberation, and he liked the smell. Here's an article that I wrote for *Gay Power* shortly after Ray's bust. After it appeared, he asked me to call him Sylvia.

Once upon a time, there existed a hotcha kingdom called Forty-second Street. It glittered and glistened with diamond-studded cats and floozy chorus girls. Dick Powell sang of it, Ruby Keeler went tip-tap-toeing down it, Busby Berkeley glorified it, and Walter Winchell orchided it. That was yesterday.

To Ray Rivera, Forty-second Street is a dying flower. "Six years ago, when I came out, the kids called Forty-two our living room, Port Authority our bathroom, and Central Park our bedroom. No more. We've lost our living room and our bedroom. We've got only our bathroom left," said Ray Rivera, the evening after his bust on West Forty-second. Ray was out petitioning—gathering signatures for the Gay Activists Alliance anti-discrimination petition that will be presented to Councilwoman Carol Greitzer.

Lily Law said, "Move." Before he knew it, Ray was riding

in a shiny new police car, on his way to the Fourteenth Precinct. He was accompanied by three officers, one of whom told Ray, "I wish you all the luck in the world because you need it."

Luck from the cops isn't what Ray needs. Ray needs love. But in the meantime, here's what Ray has.

Ray Rivera was born eighteen years ago in the Bronx. He'll never know who his father was, and doesn't remember Mama. She died when Ray was three. Luckily, there was a maternal grandmother, a salty old lady from Caracas, Venezuela, who brought up Ray in Jersey City and coped with the growing kid in her own special way, teaching him about white magic and black magic and spiritualism and prayers.

At the age of twelve, while most of us were celebrating our first pubic hairs, Ray made his debut on Forty-second Street. Coming out was good, but staying out was better. Ray listened to the beat, and preferred the music of Forty-two to the Muzak of Jersey. He got a street name, Sylvia, and he made friends. The Duchess, Josie, the penniless kids from Phoenix with cowboy hats and high hopes, the whores, the hustlers, the big umbrella of little people that sip coffee at Horn and Hardart, that share their hotel rooms at the Peerless with the passing trade, and with each other. There's a whole family thing on Forty-two, a love-hate relationship at its purest. You're up one day, you're in the money, you tell everyone you know about your good fortune, and you help them that needs help. Next day you're broke, and it's your turn to get a little help from your friends.

Forty-two wasn't, and isn't all of Ray's life. He has a job, and he had a lover. Ray works at a chain store warehouse in Jersey City. He works the night shift, 11 P.M. to 7 A.M.,

Accounts Payable, Sundays through Thursday. His take-home pay is $67.00 a week. Most mornings he comes home and sleeps through the day. He's had his job for two years.

Ray's love life has not been so good. He had a man. Ray loved him and still does. Together they slugged through a five-year relationship, featuring chaos, fidelity, infidelity, separation, reconciliations, the street, the game. Ray's guy married a dame a couple of months ago and Ray took that quick toboggan from the heights and found loneliness at the bottom of the hill. It wasn't easy.

This past March he found out about Gay Activists Alliance through the pages of *Gay Power*. He started coming to meetings. He liked what he heard. GAA became the big thing in his life, it was filling a void, it was giving Ray a cause, a reason for being, a reason to feel alive again. He talked GAA to his friends on Forty-two. "When I go to meetings," he said, "I feel a weight being lifted off my head." He urged them to join. He told everyone within earshot of this group that not only believed in the liberation of all homosexuals but was actively involved in a fight to liberate. Ray joined that fight. He participated in a couple of street actions, then took to the streets with the Greitzer petition.

I met Ray on Forty-two a day or two after his arrest. It was a warm Saturday afternoon, and hundreds of people crowded the streets, straight from the trains and buses that dumped them there. They saw this gutsy kid, with the auburn hair and the Sophia Loren almond-shaped eyes, plopped in front of the pizza place next to the Apollo Theater. They looked, and they heard "Please sign a petition to help change the laws against homosexuals." Many stopped and signed. A few asked questions. Several wished Ray luck, and one or two made caustic remarks, like "New

York is fag city." It was street theater, glamorous, vital, and surfacely appealing.

I talked to some of Ray's friends. The Duchess said, "I was here when Sylvia was arrested. She was getting signatures on her petition. The TPF came, they dragged her away. I said, 'Let her go,' but they just grabbed her and pulled her. Josie saw it, and Freddie and Steve. Ask them. It was the only action on the street that night."

Freddie said, "I hollered, 'She's only trying to circulate a petition about discrimination against homosexuals.' They took her to jail because she was only trying to do something for her people. Sylvia's a nice kid. She never bothers anybody. She's not like some of those fucking fags who are loud and ain't got nothing to give ya."

The way Ray tells it, the arrest took place on Wednesday, April 15, about 7:30 P.M. Forty-second Street was swarming with members of the Tactical Patrol Force because of the moratorium disruptions that took place earlier at Bryant Park down the street. The TPF were up tight, tighter than usual. A few people were gathered around Ray waiting to sign his petition when an overzealous TPF sweetheart asked him to move. Ray said he would as soon as the person who was signing had finished. The TPF'er told Ray he was under arrest for disorderly conduct and for trying to create a riot. Ray was led to a police car, taken to the Fourteenth Precinct, kept there an hour, not told of his civil rights, and told to plead guilty to a charge of disorderly conduct. Ray refused. He said he wasn't guilty of disorderly conduct. Bail was posted at $50.00, later changed to $25.00, and a trial date set for May 21.

The fact is, petitioning is within a person's constitutional rights, and harassment of homosexuals is the crime. Ray had the guts, the honesty to cut through the police threats and stand on his civil rights.

Knowing Ray Rivera is to be touched by him. He's a complex person, a mixture of several diverse elements, each pulling a different way. Somehow Ray aspires for the worst of heterosexual values, yet is unable to play out the house-and-garden myth. He's forthright about his homosexuality, and being gay, religious, and promiscuous are all mixed up and intertwined together. Of religion, Ray, who is a Catholic, says, "I have my own way of doing things. I have an altar at home and light candles and say prayers. Sometimes I promise my saints something, and then I try to follow through. I'm not a hypocrite and don't go to church. If I did, I'd go to a Pentecostal church. Their sermons really turn me on. I like to see happiness. The Bible says, 'Sing to God and make noise.' That's me."

The following is a note that Ray Rivera wrote to *Gay Power*:

HI, THERE:

I want to tell you a little about a new gay group. The Gay Activists Alliance. I really want to talk to my sister queens. So girls, pay me a little mind.

Well, girls, many of us were waiting for a group like GAA. I knew many of us when we used to talk about the day we could get together with other gays and be heard and ask for our freedom and our rights.

Well, sisters, the time and days are here and Gay Activists Alliance is here to stay. We are here to stop all the discrimination and police harassment and to change laws

for the gays. We want the complete liberation of all homosexuals.

We have many committees, and many things that we
are working at and we must keep on working to liberate the
gays. But you will really enjoy yourself because you're doing
it for a cause and that's the gay cause.

So girls, don't be afraid to come and see us. Because I
want to let you all know we are welcome here at GAA. The
members are all right, they don't put down no one because
they act different or wear make-up. We are all gay. Girls,
we are needed! So come on down to the Church of the Holy
Apostles, Ninth Avenue at 28th Street, Thursdays at 8
P.M. See you soon,

SYLVIA

Sylvia weaved in and out of my life during the fall and
winter of 1970. His attitudes about gay liberation—and
mine—were to change considerably in the months that
followed.

BY MAY GAA had become "the" homosexual group, and our reputation was building up a membership. The Thursday night meetings were packed to capacity. The news and television breaks of the City Hall and Snake Pit incidents, plus coverage in *Gay* and *Gay Power*, were bringing people into the organization who had never before dreamed of congregating with their own kind outside of a gay bar or their own living room. Our membership skyrocketed to one hundred, then one fifty, then two hundred, then over. We were political, we were exciting, and, to some degree, we were fun.

The publicity committee had built itself into a well-functioning unit, but chairing that committee and reporting GAA news for *Gay Power* meant a conflict of interests for me. As publicity chairman I was responsible for feeding information to media, and often the information that I had was exclusive and should have been used exclusively in *Gay Power*. I consequently found myself giving scoops and quotes to the *Gay* and the *Village Voice* reporters. As publicity chairman I wanted to see GAA news reported extensively, but as a reporter I felt peeved that it was often my exclusives that were being quoted. I decided to take off my publicity hat in early May and wear only the reportage hat.

Paul, shortly after, resigned from his chairmanship of

the political action committee. He said he was devoting too much time to the cause. Marty Robinson took over as political action chairman. Marty, in the meantime, moved out of the apartment he shared with Jim, to Tom Doerr's pad just around the corner. Tom was the blond artist who thought up the lambda as the GAA insignia. Marty had been "seeing" Tom on a regular basis, as they used to say in *Life* magazine.

Since sex was not forthcoming from Paul, I, too, started "seeing" an occasional GAA neophyte on nights off. I enjoyed being with Phil Raia, whom I had first noticed at the Lindsay TV zap. And I spent some time with a sculptor on an Esalen kick, who was instrumental in pushing me toward a weekend group encounter in New Jersey.

The encounter session was being given by Don Clark as part of his Natural Man Workshop. It was strictly a closed group for male homosexuals. There were eight of us, ranging in age from twenty-one to fifty, in background from lower middle class to upper middle class, in profession from medical student to concert pianist, in hangups from gross rejection to crawling back to the womb. We acted out our respective hangups in psychodramas.

Until the last few hours, I observed loads but contributed little. I participated in the dyads and commented on the joys and sorrows of my fellow groupies, but did not undergo an action drama of my own.

On the afternoon of the last day, the youngest member of the group, who had recently lost his father, played a scene with the oldest member of the troupe, who enacted his dead father. The older man lay motionless on the living-room floor while the young man poured forth about never living up to his father's expectations, wanting to please him, not knowing how, trying and failing time and time again. As the young man spoke, his eyes filled with tears and his body throbbed, his voice became choked; and I looked around the room, and everyone was in an emotional tizzy, including Don Clark. Everyone but me.

Don asked each of us to pinpoint his reaction to the scene that had taken place. When he came to me, I said that I was happy to see the young man spill it all out, and that it was good that everyone there received a response from the scene. However, I couldn't get emotionally involved, because pleasing my father was never a conscious problem. My problem, if that's what it's called, is that my parents tried too hard to please me, but often in the wrong fashion.

Don then asked if I'd be willing to take a trip back to my past. He asked me to close my eyes and to lean my head against the wall and to conjure up my earliest memories of my parents. I thought it was silly at first and said I could not see my parents as flesh and blood people but could see a photograph of them on the beach at Coney Island with little four-year-old me. I told Don that my earliest memory was being lost on that beach. I was rescued by a lifeguard and brought to the lifeguard's stand and held there until my parents found me. I was terrified, I said. That emotion is still vivid. I remember telling this story so often, however, that I could no longer know whether it was true or make believe.

Then, in a hypnotic state, Don took me on a journey through childhood. I went back through later incidents, some of which had been blocked out of my mind for years. It was as though a third voice had taken over deep inside, revealing forgotten secrets. Specifically I brought up a time when I was fifteen or sixteen and my father walked out on my mother, and I was sent to look for him. I remember my mother crying in the bedroom, and I remember knowing that my brother was also searching for my father, and that my sister was too young to realize what was happening. And finally, after a bit about my unsatisfactory relationship with Paul, and my more than unsatisfactory relationship with the man before him, I broke down and wailed, "I guess I'm just a lost child on the beach in a big world." Don told me to say it again and again, and I ultimately felt drained and remarked to Don, "O.K., I've said it, now what do I do?" And he answered, "Nothing, just as long as you know it, as long as you know it." And I thought, Of course I know it, but what do I do?

The encounter catharsis, unfortunately, lasted but a few days and by the end of that week I was back bemoaning the Paul plight but nevertheless sleeping with him and getting my sex elsewhere, doing my Random House job when I wasn't out confronting politicians and zapping Carol Greitzer at the Village Independent Democrats Club.

On Monday, May 11, Jim Owles finally visited Carol Greitzer at City Hall. His visit was "by appointment," and according to Jim, the gist of their conversation was that Mrs. Greitzer didn't want to have anything to do with GAA or fair employment of homosexuals. Our lady of hope and dreams said she was already involved with women's rights. She would neither sponsor nor co-sponsor a bill on homosexual discrimination, nor would she testify at the City Human Rights Commission. To quote Jim, "She was icy cold. She gave me the impression that she was taking bad medicine."

The bad medicine acted as a laxative two evenings later, when thirty-five members confronted Mrs. Greitzer at an open meeting at the Village Independent Democrats Club. It was a particularly interesting action for me, having just returned from the encounter workshop. (Although zaps may not have the long-range therapeutic value of a series of sessions with an analyst, they do tend to release poison gases and clear the head. It might be an interesting study to check out this particular form of activism therapy, if it hasn't already been done.)

Mrs. Greitzer, bereft of her City Hall shackles, is completely unprepared for the zap. Before entering the club she chats with a couple of VID people in the hallway— small talk with an air of belabored cynicism. "Who's there?" "Oh, not again." "What am I doing here?" Then she enters, and all hell breaks loose.

Marty Robinson lashes into her. "Listen, Carol, baby, you're anti-homosexual," he shouts, "anti-homosexual. Greitzer's anti-homosexual."

Grietzer fidgets. She goes to the telephone. She takes a pill from her purse and swallows it without water. She tells a VID representative that she is going to leave. She is persuaded to hear it out. She takes a deep breath and walks to the speakers' stand. And before she has a chance to open her mouth, Paul Cliffman yells, "Carol Greitzer refused to accept our petitions. Mrs. Greitzer refused to look at them. She said she would not sponsor a job discrimination bill to the Human Rights Commission. If she doesn't relate to the homosexual cause, the Village Independent Democrats don't relate, and we are prepared to sit in."

Mrs. Greitzer turns to Bob Egan, the VID president, and

says under her breath, "I don't want to talk. Tell them I have a terrible cold. I didn't refuse those petitions. I told them I couldn't take them home that day. I had too many things to carry. Tell them I have a cold and the mike isn't working. This is a charged atmosphere, and they have to be quiet if I'm going to speak to them."

Egan persists: "You've got to speak." Carol Greitzer reneges. Her eyes are now darting angry flashes. She speaks. "If your president had left them there, I'd have taken the petitions home," she says. "I saw the petitions, I accepted his word when he said that there were six thousand signatures. The City Council is not going to be able to move in any way on such petitions." Commotion from the floor. More "Carol baby's" from Marty. Bob Egan says, "Let Mrs. Greitzer finish her statement."

Mrs. Greitzer goes on. "The attorney general is the person who has done most this past year with civil rights legislation. There are other people running who can get the attorney general to introduce several pieces of legislation. There are no bills introduced through City Council. I can't get it done."

"You refuse to represent us in City Council?" queries Marty.

Mrs. Greitzer says, "Is there a specific piece of legislation you're talking about?"

Paul Cliffman replies yes and elaborates the points in the petition.

Greitzer retorts, "My stand is there is no way of getting this through our democratic process—not even with bombs."

Jim Owles says, "The very least we expect is a commitment, Mrs. Greitzer. In the past you've been accused of being anti-gay. You've never issued a positive statement about homosexuals. You are guilty of a crime of silence."

The GAA glee club joins in. "Guilty of a crime of silence."

Jim continues. "You have made statements against the war, you've made statements supporting the Women's Lib movement, supporting the blacks. Fight for us, too. Fight for us, or we'll look elsewhere."

"I'm never going to speak to anyone from this group without having a witness," says Mrs. Greitzer in front of one hundred witnesses, "because the fact is, everything I say is being misrepresented. If you ever want such legislation, you will have to have grounds for it. Gather your documents about specific cases of job discrimination. There is a right and wrong way of presenting this data to the Human Rights Commission."

"Will you back us up?" asks Marty.

"Yes," says Carol Greitzer, a look of damn-it crossing her face.

"Will you co-sponsor a bill?"

"Yes," says Carol Greitzer in a tone that can only be described as exasperated defeat.

"Do you accept the petitions?"

"Yes," says Carol Greitzer, who has one arm free for lugging that night.

At that point a warm-hearted motherly Village Independent Democrat says, "We'll go out of our way to support you. The VID is sorry that this happened. We understand why you are here. We'll do everything in our power to help you in your job discrimination fight. The channels are open and will remain open."

Carol Greitzer bites her lower lip.

At the close of our group encounter, one of our young daring members approaches Mrs. Greitzer in front of the club and asks if she'd affix her name to one of the petitions. Carol Greitzer says, "I really don't have your problem." She crosses the street and heads uptown.

And Paul and I say good night to our friends and head toward his apartment, Paul's voice sore after an evening of zapping with his most unfavorite city councilwoman.

My EDITOR, John Heys, called a meeting of the *Gay Power* staff at his downtown loft on a sunny Saturday afternoon in May. The paper was in financial difficulty. *Gay Power* needed a change of format: less organizational news and more news of a general nature to the homosexual community. The paper would abolish its centerfold double-spread nudie and genital shots. This sort of "art" tended to discourage advertisers.

John's news didn't hold too well with GAA, but the organizational political reportage was getting a good play in *Gay*, which had a bigger circulation than *Gay Power*, and several major GAA actions were being picked up by the establishment press. Anyway, the Carol Greitzer zap story was my last political piece for *Gay Power*. I followed the Greitzer story with a report on a fund-raising party that Barbra Streisand gave at her new home for Bella Abzug, the super-duper "gut" politician running for Congress who had spoken out on homosexual rights:

Sadie, Sadie, married lady, played second fiddle to Bella, Bella the pride of Gay Activists Alliance, at a gala, gala. . . . It was fascinating to see the similarities and contrasts between the show biz lady who has the money and the political lady who needs the money. They could have come from the same family, the same background, they are

74

both "their own girls," both outspoken, warm, not especially vulnerable, pushy, sincere, and likeable. Barbra can afford the best advisers and looked a vision in a polka-dot longuette, white stockings, little white buckles on little white shoes. Bella showed the wear and tear of shaking too many hands at too many subway stops. She looked nervous and frazzled and her white stockings weren't bought at the same store where Barbra shopped for hers.

I also covered Mae West at the New York opening of *Myra Breckinridge* for both *Gay Power* and the *East Village Other:*

> Up close, and I was up close, the face was that of an ancient child—Margo in *Lost Horizon*. To touch that face was to touch an illusion. To look at that face was to look at a mask that had been repaired a thousand times over with the finest glue and spit and now the glue was overshadowing the mask. Was there ever a real Mae West? How much more glue could the new Mae West take?

All of a sudden I began to hear from non-movement friends whom I had long lost touch with. "How fabulous. Mae West and Barbra Streisand. Divine."

As a follow-up, I thought it might be fun to interview Hedy Lamarr, but Miss Lamarr would have none of it. So instead I plunked myself at the head of the stairs of the Continental Baths wrapped in a terrycloth towel and asked the stalwarts to tell me what they were doing there, ha, ha, and why. I got a story out of that called "The Continental Hadassah." The title comes from a quote by a Continental employee: "The baths play a role similar to the role that Hadassah plays for Jewish women. It encases the homosexual. It makes him secure and free. It's always more comfortable to be among people you know and relate to, and it's easiest to relate physically. The Continental gives you a feeling of safety and security."

With "The Continental Hadassah" I abandoned the Arthur Irving pseudonym and wrote my first gay article under my real name. Unfortunately, the article appeared in the next to last issue of *Gay Power*, under John Heys's editorship. When he left, so did I. Shortly thereafter I began writing movie reviews for *Gay*, and very soon after that, I wrote a series of articles of a homosexual bent for the *Village Voice*.

During the late spring and early summer months I met a few good GAA people that I could talk to on a nonpolitical basis. I spent many good moments with Phil Raia, in and out of his Christopher Street apartment. Phil had taken over the pleasure committee from Ron Diamond, who was his closest friend. Both Phil and Ron were attuned to the heart of the gay movement, if not its political pulse. They kept abreast of the street news, often making news themselves. Phil was arrested one evening for sitting on a front porch stoop on Christopher Street. He called Bella Abzug from the police station to ask for legal help, and Bella, bless her, pulled strings and had a lawyer at court to represent Phil the following morning.

I was particularly fond of Michael Morrissey, who was close to Jim Owles at the moment. Michael, too, was a Christopher Street person, although he was living with his mother in New Jersey at the time. Michael was twenty when I met him. How can I describe Michael? He was serene, very much his own man, someone who was always there in a pinch. Michael came from a religious Catholic family. He attended parochial school, spent two years in college, studied acting, stowed away aboard a ship to Martinique, and participated in the Stonewall riots. He had an amazing knowledge of films and an affinity for outrageous fashions, and with his movie-star face and body he could wear anything. It was not surprising that people were constantly falling in love with him.

I got to know Michael a lot better after he broke up with Jim. He literally lived at New York University during the gay occupation that was to take place in September. He was also a leader of the group that picketed outside Republican State Committee headquarters during Gay Pride Week. And he helped me through a rough period at the end of the GAA year.

Gay Pride Week took place from June 22 to June 28. The week was to mark the first anniversary of the Stonewall riots, and was to culminate in a Gay-In at Central Park. Unfortunately, I had to leave town the day before the Gay-In—I set up a Publishers for Peace booth at the American Library Association Convention in Detroit—but stayed around for the rest of the week's GAA activities, which included an erotic art show at Frank Thompson's Art Gallery, a Fund-raising screening (the film was *Gold Diggers of 1933*), a spectacular dance at the Weinstein Hall sub-basement at NYU, and the sit-in at Republican State Committee headquarters to protest Governor Rockefeller's inaccessibility and his refusal to answer gay demands.

The *Gold Diggers* screening was poorly attended, but it

fell early in the week and wasn't well publicized. We didn't make money. The erotic art show included live nude sculptures—two men in front of a fireplace, "at home." The art, both dead and alive, was enjoyably phallic.

We hit a peak with the Republican State Committee headquarters sit-in. We had tossed around the idea of sitting in at Governor Rockefeller's headquarters, but the building was closely guarded, whereas Republican State Committee headquarters was quite accessible.

We moved in with a flurry shortly after noon on June 24. Paul, Marty, Tom Doerr, Jim, Phil Raia, Cary Yurman (a member who was the news reporter for *Gay*), one or two other people, and me.

A flunky greeted us at the door with double talk. "If you have legitimate grievances," he said, "I will see to it that they are forwarded to the right party."

"We want Rockefeller to come out and fight for homosexual rights," said Paul. "Rockefeller is guilty of a crime of silence, and we are not leaving until we get a satisfactory answer to our demands."

The flunky bleated, "You did not call for an appointment. You have not made a legitimate request."

So we just unwound and made ourselves comfortable on the floor of the reception room until they got the picture. Eventually the financial director of the Republican State Committee entered and said that the person to see was the state chairman, Charles Lanigan, but that Lanigan was out of town and unable to be reached. He suggested we write a letter asking for an appointment. We refused. We said we'd sit in until an appointment was arranged.

While we sat and sat and sat, a GAA picket line demonstrated outside the building. The line was not without incident. One man tried to assault a demonstrator and was restrained by the police. Another, slightly off his rocker, screamed at the demonstrators from down the block, which was good for bringing attention to the picket platoon, but bad for the man's lungs. As the afternoon wore on, the picket kids became more demonstrative. They held hands, kissed, hugged, quite a sight for East Fifty-sixth Street. Every half hour an upstairs sit-in would report to the crowd below, "Nothing is happening, carry on."

And nothing was happening. The television and news media crashed and took shots of the sit-ins chatting and passing around lukewarm Cokes and egg salad sandwiches brought in by understanding worn-out demonstrators. There was a definite communication gap with the Republican State Committee crew, so we amused ourselves by communicating with each other. Our only friend was the switchboard operator.

At five P.M., checkout time, the offices could not be closed. We refused to leave and were told by the financial director that copies of our demands had been sent to the governor's office and to the leaders of the State Senate and the State Assembly. "Answers cannot be created now," he said. "There are too many people involved. As far as we're concerned, we've gone as far as we can for the present moment. Nothing can be accomplished by your remaining in this office." But we sat.

At 6:30 P.M. Chairman Lanigan was finally reached by phone. He was about to board a plane for Albany. He agreed to meet with one representative of GAA at the airport before he left. Jim Owles said he'd do it providing a member of the press be allowed to come along. Lanigan refused. Jim refused to compromise. Lanigan took off for Albany, and twenty minutes later we were told by the police, who by then had joined us in the reception room, that we either leave immediately or face arrest for trespassing. A hurried meeting was called by the sit-ins, and it was agreed that Paul Cliffman, Jim Owles, Phil Raia, Marty Robinson, and Tom Doerr would pay the piper, thus becoming the first homosexuals ever arrested for a gay sit-in in New York.

Cary Yurman and I scooted downstairs to tell the crowd what was happening. A police van was parked near the building door. Within minutes the five were taken to the van and hauled off to the local police station. Eventually they'd have to appear at Criminal Court, where charges would be pressed. I suggested to the picketers that we show strength by appearing at court when they were arraigned. That would probably be in an hour or two. I also suggested that we get to the phones and call our friends to come to court and show their support for the Rockefeller Five. By eight P.M. we had forty people at Criminal Court. When the Five appeared, we stood up and held hands. This caused a flurry. The Five were then booked on a charge of criminal trespass, but were let free on their own recognizance and told to return August 5 for trial. Outside Marty Robinson told the New York *Post* reporter, "We are trying to use political power to achieve changes that will benefit homosexuals in the state. We want homosexuals to know who has been responsible for inaction regarding their civil rights, and we also wish to charge the state with corruption, such as the State Liquor Authority's non-issuance of licenses to gay bars." It got printed.

We climaxed the day by walking a few blocks to China-town, where we partook of won ton soup and fortune cookies that prophesied a good day today but rain and clouds in store tomorrow.

Friday's Gay Pride Week dance at the Weinstein Hall sub-basement of New York University brought $1500 to the GAA till. The room is mammoth and it was decorated with what looked like the remainders of Bloomingdale's Valentine's Day windows. The place fairly glittered and gleamed with cellophane and angel's hair and streamers and ribbon, and we had go-go boys on a makeshift stage and accouterments that would have made Mike Todd turn green—well, khaki—with envy.

The music started live, but the sound equipment wasn't good, so we switched to records and tapes, and someone finally brought in a super stereo, and by midnight the basement was bouncing with the sound of music and the dancing feet of the Gay Is Proud brigade. My own feet were dancing, but not too merrily that particular night. Paul Cliffman met someone at the dance and in the spirit of Gay Is Proud was demonstrating his affection toward his new acquaintance in the gayest and proudest manner. I was angry and hurt and consequently smoked too damned many reefers and kidnaped a quiet, mystical Hinduish type to a nearby friend's apartment and told him the whole sordid story of my life in two hours, then, at his request, returned to the dance feeling somewhat better. At the sight of Paul and Scarlett O'Hara I felt rotten again and, like a spoiled child, threw off my shoes and danced every remaining dance until the lights went on at five o'clock, then left with Paul, not saying a word to him about what was bothering me. If he detected a sordid purple spot in my sunny yellow disposition, he wasn't talking. The same old shit.

I left for Detroit early the next day. The American Library Association convention was fun and I saw a lot of people I knew in and out of publishing. The Publishers for Peace booth was one of the busiest there: we passed out tons of literature. The second day of the convention a member of the Social Responsibilities Round Table Committee handed me copies of a pamphlet which he asked me to distribute at the table. The stencilled sheet was headed GAY LIB POWER and read, "To our homosexual brothers and sisters: Everyone else is trying to liberate themselves. Come out! Free your profession! Free your bodies and minds! Love is beautiful! Gay is beautiful! We have a lot of potential power in the profession! Let's rap! Let's get together! Peace and love. [signed] Gay Liberation Caucus."

The pamphlet went like hotcakes, and there was much discussion at the booth from the straight librarians about the Gay Liberation Caucus. It was too near home for one of the relief people, a closeted gay editor at a well-known publishing house. He dumped the pamphlets, under the pretext that they were distracting attention away from the Publishers for Peace material. Actually, the booth was a distribution point for all material relative to the war in Asia and the unrest in America. We had tons of Women's Lib material and anti-war pamphlets from sundry groups outside the publishing profession. The pamphlets were quickly reinstated, and the Gay Liberation Caucus had fifty librarians in attendance at their first meeting held the following night, at which they discussed the need to protect librarians' opportunities for employment regardless of sexual orientation.

That same day, I received a letter from a new member of Gay Activists Alliance, whom I had gotten to know slightly before leaving New York. His name was Eben Clark, and here is his letter:

June 27, 1970

DEAR ARTHUR,

I have just returned from the Gay Liberation Day March and I want to get this off to you before the spell is broken. The weather couldn't have been more beautiful. Lots of sun, no clouds, and what I call a Suzy Parker breeze . . . just enough to gently toss the hair around. One of those few days when the air is clean of pollution and breathable. At Sheridan Square a fellow from GLF said the parade was forming at Sixth Avenue. He also told the crowd not to wear glasses in the parade and to remove any loose jewelry we might be wearing around our necks just in case someone should attack us. We walked toward Sixth Avenue, making our way through the local straights who had come out for the show. The police had to put up barricades along the street to separate the onlookers from the marchers. The crowd was small and rather nervous. Half of the gays were on the sidewalk side of the barricades, watching or trying to make up their minds about joining the march. The other half were in the street with banners and placards. The police came over and told our group to join the parade or move on. We joined. The parade started out late as usual. I think they were waiting for more people to show up. When we did get going, we got going fast. The onlookers were cool and by the time we hit the fifties all was glorious. A lot of people joined the parade along the march so when we entered Central Park we were about six blocks long. The march had a beautiful effect on my head. At first it was a little strange marching up the center of Manhattan shouting, "I'm gay. I'm gay." But as we marched it became like saying, "Hey, Mom, I'm gay and I'm beautiful." "Hey, Dad, I'm gay and I'm proud." "Hey, boss . . ." "Hey, mailman . . ." "Hey, movie star . . ." It was like dropping a heavy package you had been carrying for years and never really knowing why. We held hands and kissed and hugged each other not as exhibitionists but as friends who were sharing their freedom and pride. We became so light the breeze carried us. We marched into Sheep Meadow, home of the first Be-In, greeted by the cheers of those who had already arrived. They had marched up the hill and turned to face us chanting, "Together! Together! Together!" And "together" we were. It was our day and the sun was shining for us. The day was then broken down into smaller events. Cary Yurman broke the world's kissing record, GAA set up some games, GLF rapped with some of the media that had arrived for the celebration. I didn't see much of Mattachine. A friend and I rolled in the grass, blew a few joints and existed on the pleasures of the day. We greeted other friends with hugs and outrageous shouts. We danced and ran around until the sun decided to go down. We knew the day had ended but the work had just begun. We moved back through that mysterious warp that had allowed us to escape our brainwashed heads and joined the summer tourists on Fifth Avenue.

I wish you were there to celebrate with us. Come home soon.

E<small>BEN</small>

Of course I read about the march in *The New York Times* and saw part of it on television in Detroit. When I did come home, July 4, I was told how glorious it was, how successful it was, how uplifting it was. Gay had made it in a big way.

The Thursday general meeting that followed could only be an anticlimax to Gay Pride Week, and it was. We discussed the sale of our lambda shirts and buttons to the Homophile Action League in Philadelphia, we talked about silently supporting Ray Rivera at Criminal Court at his rescheduled "petition" trial, and Jean De Vente, the butch mother-figure captain of a Riis Park Softball Team, announced that the team would henceforth be called the GAA Softball Team. We were riding high.

THE SECOND GAA dance was scheduled for July 10 at St. Peter's Church. Phil Raia and his pleasure committee in alliance with the street theater committee planned on a dance-happening, a joyous anything-goes event featuring balloons and candles and bubble machines and toffee apples and spectacular entrances and joyous disturbances in the manner of a flower child circus. The dance was to be a perfect expression of Phil's flower child nature: a nature completely incomprehensible to Marty and Jim and Paul. Phil was into dancing and loving his way to liberation.

Five days before the dance-happening Phil called a meeting of his committee at his Christopher Street apartment. About fifty people showed. We split into two groups. One stayed at Phil's to discuss the distribution of work ("I'll take care of supplying an ice pick; you buy the gypsy bubble gum"), the other moved to Ron Diamond's pad around the corner to plan "theater" for the dance. I went to Ron's along with ten or twelve regulars, including an immense heart-of-gold black transvestite named Natasha. Two new women were also in the contingent.

Natasha got down to brass tacks immediately. The week before, he had been chosen Miss Black Universe. He and a masochistic go-go dancer thought up a happening for the dance. The dancer, dressed in leather jock strap, would tow a heavy rope onto the center dance floor. At the end of the rope would be Natasha, dressed in prize drag. Natasha would strip out of his costume, revealing the nude body of a man. He would then shoot off a gun, spilling paper flowers. The ultimate transvestite flower child anti-war trip.

As it happened, the two women at the meeting objected to the presentation. Not only was it oppressive to women, they said, it was also oppressive to blacks. Someone chimed in about the imagery of black man in ropes and bond, and one or two others agreed that the act might do with some rethinking. Natasha seemed willing enough to listen but was firm about appearing, some way, somehow, in prize-winning costume.

At the executive committee meeting that took place prior to the dance, the two women objectors approached Jim Owles with their beef. Jim arbitrarily took it upon himself to veto Natasha's drag entrance. It was a decision that he made without consulting Phil or Natasha or the membership at large. And suddenly a little *tsimmis* developed into a major issue. The issue: the autonomy of the president over the membership, and whether GAA as a political group was relating to women, transvestites, sadists, masochists, blacks, and flower children.

The dance-happening went on without Natasha's act. The night was hot and sticky and the air was thick with humidity—and some hostility. But for most the dance was a dream of perfection. Dressed like a white bunny in a folded-hankie bathing suit that barely covered his genitals, Ron Diamond handed out candies and little rings. Balloons danced in the air, and balloon-heads wiggled sweat-covered bodies to the Supremes' greatest hits. Afro wigs reached out to touch the churchtop roof and elbows went chop-chop and red suspenders held up peek-a-boo pants and necklaces jangled and grass went around the room and women in couples danced navel to navel to soul music. The kids at the door sold dozens of lambda T-shirts. The kids in the back sold dozens of cans of beer and cheap soda pop. And GAA sold dozens of dreams of liberation and kinship and love. We danced our way to heaven.

Heaven was hardly the order of the day at the Thursday meeting that followed the dance. Natasha showed up ready to kill. He led an angry army of transvestites and outraged supporters. Sylvia was by Natasha's side, as were Phil and Ron Diamond and Michael Morrissey. They disrupted the meeting. They told Natasha's side of the story and came down heavy on Jim Owles, blaming him for prejudicial, unjust, dictatorial handling of a molehill that needn't have developed into a mountain. They blamed Jim for not checking out the facts but merely going on the word of outside troublemakers. The women, they claimed, were liars and disrupters. They quoted the GAA preamble about "the right to treat and express our bodies as we will, to nurture them, to display them, to embellish them, solely in the manner we ourselves determine." Natasha, strongly supported by Phil Raia, demanded an apology from Jim Owles. No such luck. Marty Robinson, taking the role of diplomatic peacemaker—a role he didn't play too well—made matters worse by "explaining" for Jim. The evening ended with a resolution that we support and show affection for our transvestite members and support and love our president. The resolution was sanctimonious, phony and outlandish.

The power of the pleasure committee and the fear by Marty Robinson, Jim Owles, and Paul Cliffman that the people of GAA would "dance our way to liberation" resulted in a constitutional upheaval and the setting-up of a new committee structure. The goals of the organization, spelled out, would henceforth be heavily political. At a meeting that took place at St. Peter's Church, Robinson, Cliffman, and Owles represented the politicians; Phil Raia and his pleasure committee represented the social brigade. Here's how Michael Morrissey describes it:

Jim and Paul sat together and told Phil's group that they were responsible for all of the trouble at GAA and for the Natasha upset. The pleasure people, they said, couldn't work in a political system. Paul Cliffman and Jim Owles both decided that the only way the organization could survive was to split GAA into two separate groups—one would be political, keeping the GAA name and working under the GAA constitution, the other would be social. They told Phil Raia that he could take anyone who wanted to follow him to form his social working organization. Maybe sometime in the future they could form a union again, they said, but right now the social people were getting in the way of the political people. I told them that I'd just as soon carry a picket sign as carry beer and ice at a dance. In my mind it's the same thing, and it's silly to work for two separate organizations. But it became apparent that Owles and Cliffman had no idea of compromising at all. After a bit Marty walked in. He began attacking the pleasure people—he called them dead weight. Then he became patronizing and slipped into a fifteen-minute tirade against "all you people who want to dance your way to liberation." He said he

89

would leave GAA and form an elite strike group. I remember that term clearly because I thought it sounded so much like the Nazis. Paul walked out. He wasn't about to make any concessions. Shortly after, Marty left with Jim on his arm. Those of us that remained thought it was the end of GAA and decided all we could do was to play it by ear until the next general meeting. In the next day or two the Owles, Cliffman, Robinson team got on the phones and made it clear to everyone that Phil Raia was causing a split in GAA. They warned Phil that the problem couldn't get to the floor on Thursday. Obviously they were afraid he'd have the sympathy and support of the membership. And by Thursday Phil was fed up. He showed up at the meeting but said nothing. Phil slowly dropped out of GAA. When he left, a lot of people went with him. They were disgusted with the political slaughterings and ego trips of Paul Cliffman and Jim Owles and Marty Robinson.

The following week Paul, in peak form, worked out a new committee mandate, which was ultimately brought to the floor and approved by the membership. The mandate was top heavy on politics. Paul introduced a political projects committee to recommend the setting up of ad hoc committees to work on specific political projects. Marty Robinson was appointed chairman. The first of the new political committees were fair employment, elections, and police harassment. Richie Aunateau, a twenty-four-year-old ex-Democratic Party district leader who was inadvertently at the first GAA confrontation at the Village Independent Democrats Club, was appointed head of fair employment. Its mandate was to recommend strategy for demonstrations and lobbying in order to effect passage of a bill which would outlaw job discrimination against homosexuals. Richie's political knowledge and savvy inspired a committee of professionals to carry on a teamwork project that was too damned independent and perfect for the Robinson-Owles team to leave alone. As expected, trouble came at the end of the year. Marc Rubin was appointed head of the elections committee. Marc also had an extensive background in politics. He was a leader of the Bolivar-Douglas Reformed Democratic Club in the early 1960s, worked on the Mississippi Freedom Summer project, led voting demonstrations, was arrested for leafleting in Cleveland, Mississippi, worked with CORE, was involved with peace movement activities, and campaigned for Lindsay during his second mayoral race. Marc was big on the political reform aspect of GAA and was a natural leader for the election people, who were to recommend strategy for demonstrations for statewide elections that were to take place in a few months.

My friend and Gay Pride Week letter writer, Eben Clark, headed the police power committee, whose function was to recommend strategy for ending harassment by police of homosexuals at gay bars and baths. Eben is a former actor, Pasadena Playhouse graduate, china and crystal salesman at Tiffany's, anti-war demonstrator, sculptor, and fashion plate. To most of the members he was just a tall body with a thin face, beard, and long hair until this committee was formed. Eben's cognizance of what liberation is, and how best to achieve it, was to cause another Phil Raia incident, only deeper, at the end of the GAA year.

The legal committee remained unchanged but a new fair tax committee was set up to work on challenging unjust tax structures (why, for instance, couldn't a homosexual couple file a joint tax return?). A leaflet and graphics committee was set up to edit and distribute all street leaflets for GAA and its committees and to hold and operate the mimeograph machine. Tom Doerr, Marty Robinson's lover, was chosen to chair this committee, causing some concern, since the mimeo machine was to be kept in the apartment that he and Marty now shared. (Marty had been known to rewrite and distort pamphlets to his own style of thinking without first checking with the pamphlet writer.) The publicity committee underwent a name change. It was now the news committee, but its functions were primarily the same—providing media with information about GAA.

To diminish the pow of the pleasure committee, the street theater subcommittee was dropped altogether. A separate fund-raising committee was set up, and the name "pleasure" was dropped. It became social affairs. Fundraising was to solicit moneys through mass mailings, the sale of T-shirts, and commercial devices. And social affairs was to recommend dances and social events in order "to raise the political consciousness of the community" (as opposed to the social consciousness), and to promote the unity and morale of its members. Three or four benefits proposed by Phil Raia were canceled, and a political type who had never attended a pleasure committee meeting was selected to head the new social committee. Future dances would henceforth have a political theme. The first dance under social affairs would be for the Rockefeller Five.

The beginning of the final ending for Paul and me began August 5, the day of the Rockefeller Five trial. Morty Manford, Paul's fellow student at Columbia and gay power accompanist in the hallways of the Metropolitan Museum, was appointed to head a committee to publicize the Rockefeller Five trial. Morty staged a couple of rallies that were poorly attended, but put together a couple of decent pamphlets urging support of the infamous quintet: "Raise a storm of protest that every gay in the state can hear. Call your brothers and sisters to a world of gay is powerful. Let no politician remain shielded behind silence." The trial was set for a Wednesday morning at the old Ray Rivera Criminal Court camping grounds at 100 Centre Street. The usual frantic calls were made to media and a plea was put forth to GLF to join us. About one hundred activists picketed outside the courthouse ("Rocky Has a Happy, Why Can't We"), others lent their lambda-chested support to the five brothers in the stuffy courtroom. The hearing, as expected, was postponed. Nevertheless, the Rockefeller Five appeared on the courthouse steps in a gesture of political showmanship. Garbed in lambda blue and gold, looking mad as hell, making fists and clutching arms, they made a stirring sight for the CBS-TV news cameras. (Gloria Rojas to Jim Owles: "How do you explain that things that weren't mentioned before are now movements?" Jim Owles to Gloria Rojas: "It's all part of the new cultural revolution that's been brought about by many of the other minority groups.") The Five then led a procession to Foley Square, a block or two away, for speechmaking. There, camaraderie was rife, the crowd

93

jovial, vibes were good, and gay was indeed proud. At Foley, Morty Manford made a decent speech—Morty was motivated by decency—followed by a wow speech by Paul and a couple of spiels by GLF in the spirit of the day. Then Paul, Marty Robinson, Jim Owles, and I headed toward Marty and Tom's apartment. I knocked out a quick story on Marty's battered old typewriter. For the hell of it I delivered the story to the *Village Voice*.

The following week it broke on the front page. I was surprised to say the least. It began, "Gay did not die after Gay Pride Week—it just lay dormant for a month. It sprang back full force last week with a couple of actions that reached out beyond New York's homosexual community to the political arenas of both the Democratic and Republican parties." The article concluded with Paul's speech: "Today we know that gay is angry. We are telling all the politicians and elected officials of New York State that either they're going to become responsible to the people or we will go into the Legislature and the courts and the Mayor's office and the offices of the Governor and City Councils. We will make them responsible to us or else we will stop the conduct of the business of government."

I was happy with the coverage, and when I saw Paul that evening, he too was beaming and his head was racing. We ate dinner at my place and talked about how wonderful we were. So wonderful, so marvelous, in fact, that Paul said he might run against Carol Greitzer for the council seat in the next City Council election.

The possibilities of his winning were good to excellent, he thought. The percentage of gay constituents in the Greitzer area was overwhelming. Paul's charisma and political savvy would shoo him in, if the scene were set just right. First he'd have to get an apartment in the Village (a councilman must reside in the district which he councils). Then the natural thing would be to win the presidency of GAA. Thoughts were playing hockey in my head that night, and it took me hours to fall asleep. Paul, Mister Councilman; me, the faithful journalist by his side. Politics plus media equal power and love. It would work for us.

Too many bad movies and too much *Village Voice* blurred out the truth of who we really were that night. I should have seen the sowing of the ego seeds that were to blossom full fruit and explode in December.

MY FRONT PAGE "gay" story drew some attention at Random House. Several nodding acquaintances said, "Right on," and two Women's Lib sympathizers, both in children's books, asked if they could take me to lunch to discuss how the movements might relate to each other. But by and large the *Voice* story went unnoticed or was taken as part of a day's living.

Much as I loved Random House, I was finding work a hassle. I put off doing the newsletter that I was responsible for cranking out, and instead of initiating work I was allowing work to initiate elsewhere. When letters came, they lay dormant on my desk. I used my office as a liberation base and a drop-in place for friends to chew the fat. I was getting in late and leaving early, and cutting days to go to Criminal Court and to zap candidates and confront politicians. I was grinding out movement stories and now movie reviews for *Gay* on my office typewriter. I neglected the world of children's books—in fact, found it an intrusion. Once a week I'd make a five-minute appearance on the children's book floor to let them know I was alive. Most of my office work was done by my trusty and loving assistant. Nothing spectacular or imaginative was coming from me. Jean Ennis, the petite public relations lady who was my boss, sensed that my thoughts were elsewhere, but I doubt if she knew of my outside activities. Jean and I lunched a couple of times during August and September—once with a *McCalls* editor, once with a *Good Housekeeping* reviewer—but Jean never indicated that I was doing a less than sensational job, and there was no guilt from me about my ennui. I just found gay liberation more interesting and rewarding than Dr. Seuss.

At the tail end of August several gay groups (Radical Lesbians, Gay Liberation Front, Gay Activists Alliance, Gay Youth) joined forces to protest a rash of harassment on Forty-second Street. For three weeks preceding the demonstration gay people were being arrested en masse for simply "being." Typical is the case of a strait-laced, effeminate-faced acquaintance who went to the Lyric Theater on a Saturday night. On coming out he was jostled by an officer, hustled to a waiting police van, and hauled off to the Fourteenth Precinct, where he was held for fourteen hours. Why? Vagrancy, he was told. No charges were pressed, and the young man was released and warned not to show his face on Forty-second again.

On the afternoon of the demonstration twenty-five people showed up for marshal training at a Gay Liberation Front loft on West Seventeenth Street. The marshals were given instructions on how to handle demonstrators in case of a police onslaught (walk quickly, do not run), how to keep the marchers together, and what to do in case of violence. Paul Cliffman and Cary Yurman and Eben Clark were among those present, and violence was possible, in fact expected. The march was not officially sanctioned by the city—we did not have a parade permit. Hordes of homosexuals proclaiming gay power in an explosive area could mean fireworks.

As night approached we gathered at the southwest corner of Eighth Avenue and Forty-second Street. About four hundred strong with banners galore, flags and signs. A GLF pamphlet proclaimed, "The heat is on. Demonstrate to end police harassment. 300 gays busted. Pigs are raiding every gay center in the city. The Village is next. Come out."

In addition to "us" the area was swarming with "them" —newsmen, television cameramen, cops on horses, a lowly "observer" from the mayor's office, and a hundred million people in for a Saturday on the town. While we were pulling ourselves together, I introduced myself to the NBC and CBS news cameramen. Looking wild-eyed but compassionate (a very good look for TV), I talked about the reasons for the march and answered questions for the *Eleventh Hour News*. Of course, being a company man, I gave GAA top billing, mentioning GLF as an afterthought.

The march began. We walked from Eighth Avenue to Broadway, crossed Forty-second Street, and marched back to Eighth again. We blew minds! Natasha, with hair teased like never before, carried a placard: "We're the people our parents warned us against." The "Gay Power" signs were there and "Gays Unite" and "We Will Smash Your Heterosexual Culture" and "Hands Off of Our Community." We passed the *Watermelon Man* marquee and *Myra Breckinridge* and *The Filthy Five* ("loving like animals and fighting like beasts"), and as we marched, the voices grew louder and louder: "Gay is proud." "Up the pigs." "Gay power." I weaved in and out of the parade, steno pad in one hand, tape recorder in the other, squeezing out comments from passers-by, comments such as "Don't speak to me" and "I've got a father on the police force and I love him but he doesn't understand what this is all about. I do." We circled Forty-second Street three times. Each time the crowd grew larger and the sideline hecklers more boisterous. I spotted Paul now and then, hustling people along, very much in control. The last time we rounded Forty-second and Eighth, one of the "God Is Love" disciples grabbed my arm. "Let me save your soul," he said. I dropped out of line and, with tape recorder in hand, asked him "How?" Within minutes I was surrounded by Christ worshipers and onlookers (the gay parade had passed by) and was the central figure in a "soul" debate. Could mine be saved and was it worth saving? The majority opinion was no, but I didn't stay long enough to find out for sure. I wormed my way through the mob, cries of "Repent" following me, and caught up with the gay march. By then the parade had left the madness of Forty-second for the soulful dark streets leading to the Fourteenth Precinct. We planned to vocalize our anger at the precinct, making our final punctuation point, and thereafter ending the march. Close to the police station, Eben Clark was approached with a warning that the police planned to attack the crowd should we disperse then and there. So instead of coming to a stop, Eben, at the head of the march, led the crowd past the stationhouse and on to brightly lighted Thirty-fourth Street. It was done so quietly and quickly that many people didn't realize we were at the Fourteenth Precinct until we had passed it.

We continued to march. "Hey, hey, good is gay. Try it once the other way." Down deserted Seventh Avenue and toward the Village. At Thirty-first Street, near a construction site, a bottle was hurled, hitting the head of a GLF kid. At Twenty-first Street another marcher was hit, this time by a rock. Howard Blum of the *Voice* and Bob Kohler of GLF asked a Tactical Patrol Force officer to take the bleeding victim by car to St. Vincent's. He refused. This wasn't his district, he said. At Fourteenth Street Kohler told Jim Owles that the GLF contingent would continue the march to the Women's House of Detention.

"Count us out," said Owles, "we've done our duty. From here on in, the march is a GLF action."

Marty Robinson argued with Jim that we continue. Jim, this time, persisted. He left the parade and headed toward his apartment, leaving Marty, figuratively speaking, holding the GAA banner. Word went through the ranks that those GAA people marching would now march as individuals. Some left the line. Many stayed. Paul and I stayed.

As we reached Sheridan Square, the crowds swelled. We marched around the Women's House of Detention shouting joyously and boisterously, "Free the women, free the women." We ran down Christopher Street yelling Indian war whoops. We were kids doing what we've always wanted to do, and damn all inhibitions. A wild feeling of head-clearing freedom was ours. We circled Sheridan Square again. At the Haven, a unisex dance club, a badly timed freak show was in progress. The police and fire departments selected that moment to hassle the Haven's management about overcrowding. "We can't let them get away with this," said Paul. "This fucking harassment is what the march is about." Then, within two feet of the Haven's entranceway, Paul slammed his palm against the Haven wall and shouted, "Gay power." He did it again and again. Suddenly the chant was picked up. By hundreds. Deafening. "Gay power. Gay power. Gay power." The cops attacked, truncheons swinging. All hell broke loose, and we were fleeing from the enemy.

Paul and I split but found each other again near Sixth Avenue. Outside the House of Detention the chanting continued. "Free the women. Free the women." Several flaming rolls of toilet paper drifted down from the prison windows. The crowd cheered. More police arrived on the scene.

They lined the rooftops. They barricaded Eighth Street. The crowd swelled to more than two thousand. The heart of Greenwich Village was a battlefront, people against pigs.

There was violence. The police charged with night sticks. The crowd hurled missiles. There were broken bones—and blood and torn clothing and an exhilaration of the moment. And fear.

Paul and I and a few GAA friends played advance and retreat with the cops and the crowd. Children at their games, but the games were real.

In the middle of the foray we stopped for an intermission of coffee-flavored ice cream sodas at our favorite restaurant in the riot area. "Only in New York," said Paul. "Only in New York."

The following day Gay Liberation Front held a press conference at the Church of the Holy Apostles that ended in a free-for-all, and that evening a small band of outlaw gays marched to the House of Detention and roamed the Village area. Many street people condemned what they thought would be a continuation of the previous night's activities and refused to take part in the undirected demonstration There was little trouble, however—two minor skirmishes, a broken chair at O. Henry's, and several sore throats. By midnight the rains had drenched away the end-of-summer riots and the next day the cops were back on their beat, hassling homosexuals on West Forty-second Street. But with discretion.

DISCRETION IS hardly the word to describe my Baltimore adventure with Spiro Agnew's son, Randy, and his friend Buddy Hash of La Triolet Beauty Salon.

It happened as a result of an article by syndicated columnist Jack Anderson, which ran in the New York *Post* on September 5. The article began, "Vice President Agnew is deeply troubled about his son, Randy, who has broken up with his wife and has been living for the past month with Buddy Hash, a male hairdresser, in Baltimore."

Anderson's column was filled with innuendo ("Randy's nowhere near the hippie type," said Buddy Hash. "He's really very goody goody") and came at a time when Agnew Senior was blasting American youths for being brainwashed into a drug culture of rock music, movies, books, and underground newspapers ("a depressing life style of conformity that has neither life nor style") and placing part of the blame on "pill-popping parents who are setting examples for younger citizens to do some experimenting on their own."

A day or two after the Anderson article appeared, I visited my editor at *Gay* with a movie review of *Something for Everyone*. He and I talked about the case of Randy Agnew, as seen through the syndicated eyes of Jack Anderson. "Would you consider going to Baltimore to check out his story?" he asked. Without hesitation I said yes. On a non-exclusive basis.

Three days later I was on my way. I was given the phone number of the manager of a well-known disreputable establishment who was a friend of the advertising manager of *Gay* and who allegedly knew everyone in Baltimore. This man put me on to a few good leads. Eventually, I spoke to Buddy Hash at his salon. Hash said he'd meet me at six; he finally showed up at a political dance, where I was taken by his mother, at eleven. Hash, accompanied by his brother, a girl friend, and a press agent, denied that Randy Agnew was anything more than a friend. He denied being a homosexual and claimed the Anderson story was false.

The following morning, I took a bus to the suburban Towson Plaza Shopping Center. I found the Holiday Health Salon hidden in a building behind a bank—the spot where Randy Agnew worked as a weight-lifting instructor.

Getting to Randy was easy. I introduced myself to the receptionist, asked if I could speak to Mr. Agnew, and in two shakes a well-built, straight-looking, good-looking, unaffected twenty-four-year-old dreamboat appeared. I told him who I was and said I'd appreciate his comments on the implications in Anderson's column about his relationship with Buddy Hash. He answered, "They were not facts at all. When I was getting my garage fixed, there was no way of moving into it and a friend of mine said he knew of this place that Buddy had—a whole downstairs that I could use until I got myself straightened out and could move into my new place."

"How long have you known Buddy?" I asked.

"About half a year. I met him through a friend."

"Have there been any repercussions because of the column? Political repercussions? Feedback through friends?"

Randy replied, "Just people saying that it's too bad it had to come out about my separation from my wife. You don't want people to publicize anything like that. You don't want the world to know about it."

"What about repercussions on the homosexual angle?"

"Most people didn't even pick it up," said Randy, who obviously doesn't know the same people I do. "Buddy Hash is a businessman. He spends long hours at his shop. What he does after hours, I don't know."

We talked about his father's recent rantings from Wyoming on liberal radical Democrats. According to Randy, the people who talk to him directly about his father's politics usually commend his father for having the guts to make a stand.

I left Randy Agnew after thirty minutes of conversation and headed back toward Baltimore proper. Frankly, I had a delicious non-story. So I wrote up a non-story, both for the *Village Voice* ("The Randy Agnew File") and for *Gay* ("Agnew's Son Talks to *Gay*").

The *Voice* story, which concentrated mostly on the runaround I got from the Buddy Hash camp, caused much controversy. Indignant letters to the editor charged invasion of privacy. ("I doubt that the *Voice* would assign to or accept a story from a reporter about the sexual habits or proclivities, say, of Eugene McCarthy's daughter, if he has a daughter. Why not let young Agnew be? He's probably miserable enough in any case with the burden of a father about whom he had no choice.") Two pages in the October *Mattachine Newsletter* tore the story and me to shreds. And I was dropped from NBC's *Today* show, where I was scheduled for a fifteen-minute discussion on the homosexual movement. (I was booked before the article appeared. When the producer read the article, he got cold feet. Possible repercussions. They rebooked me four months later, the Agnew issue apparently dead. Incidentally, the sight of a homosexual talking about homosexuality on national television during the early morning breakfast hour caused a flurry of hate mail. More than five hundred letters came to the *Today* show, about 75 per cent negative, most of them quoting the Bible, several saying, "You'll have rapists and murderers on next.")

The Agnew story did not set back the movement ten years, as one GLF member seemed to think. It was an article written and told as it happened, and nothing more—or less.

My Random House phone rang for weeks after "The Randy Agnew File." Most of the callers wanted the lowdown: Is he or isn't he? Perhaps only his hairdresser knows. I didn't.

Diego "Tito" Vinales had dinner with me at my apartment late in the summer. He was driven by car to the city by the friend who took him to the Snake Pit, and with whom he was living in New Jersey.

Tito had put on a considerable amount of weight in the two months since leaving the hospital. "All I do is eat and watch television," he said. His face was pasty. His eyes lacked luster. His unkempt clothing made him look old and he moved with the slowness of an old man—lowering himself into a chair, shuffling, even his words were slow to come out.

He was frightened, so frightened, about deportation. Outside of his lawyer, his friend, and me, no one knew where he was living. His lawyer was working on his deportation case, but the threat of leaving America kept Tito awake at night. "I would rather die than return to Argentina."

I wanted to know why. He was frittering away his time, he admitted his life was empty. Why was it so important for him to stay.

"Coming to America," he said, "is my dream since I was a little boy. I dreamed of having a car in America and living in a beautiful building. I wanted to be rich and happy with beautiful clothing, to laugh and have many friends and go to parties. Maybe this will happen someday. For this hope I will stay in America. I still have my dream. I will never go back."

On September 17 Eben Clark began our general meeting with the announcement that Mayor Lindsay was scheduled to appear at nine P.M. that night at an anti-war demonstration. The demonstration was to be sponsored by Bridge for Peace at New York University's Loeb Student Center. Those interested in zapping the mayor were asked to leave the meeting immediately and head toward Washington Square Park. Our strategy was to try to get into the auditorium and ask the mayor those questions that he knew too well, those questions which he continued to refuse to answer personally and publicly. We were to come down heavily on police harassment again. Perhaps in front of a young liberal audience Mr. Lindsay would be forced to make a stand.

Loeb Center is packed. There isn't an empty seat in the house and they aren't letting latecomers in. I spot Bella Abzug, shout yoo hoo, and wrangle my way past the door attendant, into the auditorium and into the press room. Bella has already given her spiel. She and writer Jimmy Breslin are waiting for Lindsay, and Lindsay is late. Bella gives up and leaves.

Thirty minutes later Lindsay appears. He is jittery, having just been confronted by seventy gay activists outside the building. His ears are still ringing with "End police harassment." He goes immediately from the press room to the auditorium stage, where he is greeted by a thunderous ovation. His speech is prepared. About five minutes into it ("Each American is now a victim and a prisoner of the Vietnam war"), a familiar figure in a Columbia University pullover casually walks up to the stage, plunks himself in front of a second microphone, and says, "Pardon me for interrupting, Mr. Mayor." By God, it's Morty Manford!

"Pardon me for interrupting, Mr. Mayor, but this is the only way that we can get to you since you refuse to see us through regular channels." The feeling of the audience is that of hostility. Before Morty is recognized as a homosexual activist, he is ushered off stage by the mayor's bodyguard. Lindsay continues his speech. But now he is speaking words without meaning. The audience is restless, very much aware of the mayor's nervousness, expecting a further disruption. It happens. Ten minutes later, from out of nowhere, Morty appears at the microphone again, but this time to make his point.

"The Gay Activists Alliance has no other way to deal with police harassment in New York City," says Morty. "We must confront the mayor in public. This past month over three hundred gays were arrested in the midtown area by Lindsay's police force. How do you plan to control your police, Mayor Lindsay? Why don't you listen to your homosexual constituents?"

There is no response from Lindsay, who frantically rustles through his notes. The audience is listening. "If you can't control the police, you shouldn't aspire to the presidency," says Morty as the mayor shuffles his papers some more.

Morty leaves the stage. He is greeted by mild applause. The mayor continues his speech to an audience that has stopped listening.

Back in the press room on the way out, I ask Lindsay when he expects to meet face to face with the homosexual community. He answers that he is aware of our problems and that Michael Dontzin and Deputy Mayor Aurelio keep him up to date on our goings and comings and that we should continue to work out our problems through them. "But when will we have a face-to-face meeting?" I ask.

Lindsay answers that every minority group in town wants a face-to-face meeting and he's been in office five years and has spoken to the Jews just once and the Italians not at all and the blacks once or twice and the women for the first time only last week. When the mayor finally appears on the steps of Loeb Center on his way to his car, he is greeted with the sight of GAA surrounding the damn thing. "End police harassment, end police harassment." The mayor doesn't lose his cool—he is to be respected for his composure on the battlefield. He gets into his car and is driven into the dark abyss of the night, smiling, disgusted, and aware.

Later that night, one of the new members—a face I've never seen before—asks me to come to a meeting of the Gay Student Liberation of New York University. It's at his dormitory that Sunday. I say I will if I can. He writes down particulars. He is cute as hell and I want to bed down with him.

"Gay power, brother," he says.

"Right on, brother," I say.

And Paul and I head for home.

Sunday came. My parents were in town. I had an early dinner with them at O. Henry's. It was a "without Paul" night. I was in the Village. It was 7:30. I figured, Why not?

The New York University dormitory building on West Eleventh Street is a stone fortress without character. One of the NYU gay students whom I had seen around before and spoken to once or twice spotted me looking for the meeting room.

"This is a private meeting," she said. "Are you here as an individual or as a reporter or member of GAA?"

"As an individual," I replied, thinking the old paranoia game.

Inside, the cute-as-hell kid wasn't around. I spotted a couple of other familiar figures, though, including Martha Shelley, the big-boned earthy Radical Lesbian writer-activist. Martha questioned me about my motives for being there. It was a scene from *The Iron Curtain*. I passed the screen test. The meeting began.

Martha, in an open shirt and work trousers, chaired. The subject wasn't roses; it was New York University, the relationship of its facilities to the community in which it is located, and the refusal of the university to open its facilities for dances to a recognized student group, the Gay Student Liberation of NYU.

It seems that after our smash GAA dance in June the Christopher Street Liberation Day Committee worked out a deal with the student body Weinstein House Commission to hold four dances in the air-conditioned sub-basement. Two dances were held. But by the time the third dance was to take place, administration, lo and behold, got wind of the fact that homosexuals were using school facilities. They told the Christopher Street Committee that the dances would be canceled. Students have control of Weinstein facilities, they indicated, but there are limits.

Administration was able to fall back on the fact that the Christopher Street Liberation Day Committee was not a bona fide student group. Realizing what was being pulled, the Gay Student Liberation of NYU offered to sponsor or co-sponsor the two remaining Christopher Street dances. Their offer prompted Vice Chancellor Harold Whiteman to remark that New York University was unsure of the "validity" of the life style of homosexuals. Gay dances on the campus would affect "impressionable freshmen."

Whiteman continued that it would be best to submit the topic of homosexuality to a panel of ministers and psychologists—learned men who would deal with gay on the sickness theory.

On the night of the scheduled third dance, several dozen homosexuals appeared in front of Weinstein Hall with picket signs. Administration, caught by surprise, feared violence and opened the hall. The following week they canceled the last of the scheduled dances. The cancellation went without incident. Administration, however, also discussed revoking the charter of the Gay Student Liberation of New York University. Punishment.

The question posed by Martha Shelley and the NYU group that night of September 20 was Do we go along with a veto decision by the power structure or do we turn their decision into a Morningside Heights-Columbia University issue—an issue of relationship between university and community? The majority opted for a sit-in at Weinstein.

"Let's do it tonight," said Martha Shelley, half in jest. "Why not," said an NYU student, in dead seriousness. So with nowhere to go, and with only one foot in the door, I began a week of commune living and head changing. After Weinstein, GAA was no longer the open sesame to homosexual liberation. People were—not constitutions or brand names.

Martha and I wrote a pamphlet. "Help us now! Despite the fact that NYU is located in the world's largest gay ghetto, its facilities are closed to the gay community. Administration has made a moral judgment about what it considers a valid life style. Who gave them the right to judge us? We are occupying Weinstein sub-cellar tonight and will not relinquish it. Support your gay brothers and sisters. Join us."

A crew of four cranked out the pamphlet on a mimeo machine, then took to Christopher Street and Sheridan Square to distribute it and to round up the street people. The woman who headed the NYU gay student group raced to the Gay Liberation Front meeting, which was then in progress, to report our doings and to ask that all of the people there leave and head straight for Weinstein. Meanwhile, Martha Shelley and I headed for the sub-basement.

It was deserted, except for a ping-pong game for two. "We'll play when you're finished," said Martha. "Leave your rackets." They left. We stayed.

An hour later the first crew arrived: Michael Morrissey and Sylvia and the street people. Then about forty men and women from the Gay Liberation Front came in. At that point I headed toward a phone to call AP, UP, the *Times*, the *Post*, the *Daily News*, and the radio and television stations. I was told by Martha to read the pamphlet only and not to answer questions. I also called the movement lawyers.

The air was sticky and oppressive outside, but downstairs in the air-conditioned womb the spirit was buoyant. Someone played "Silent Night, Holy Night" on the piano. Someone had a record player. Some danced. And Martha Shelley said, "I think we should stay until we all grow long beards."

The following day some short gay stubbles were seen in the upstairs corridors. The sit-ins had taken to the dorm floors to speak to the men and women student residents about our demands and to answer questions about "Why the occupation?" Talk, talk, talk, on the dorm steps, in bunk beds, in the cafeteria, buzz, buzz, buzz, gay rights, administration, justification, stepping on toes, chartered group, support, equality, liberation.

That night a vote was taken, and a representative from each dorm floor was sent to a general meeting presided over by the director of the Weinstein dormitory governing body. Most of the "impressionable freshmen" were concerned about student rights, which now coincided with gay rights. They were pissed off about the fact that administration went over their heads negating the House Commission's authority to rent out Weinstein's facilities as the dorm residents saw fit. The floor vote went two to one in favor of supporting the rights of the Gay Student Liberation of NYU to enjoy equal privileges with all other recognized student organizations. Another outcome was that the use of the facilities of Weinstein would continue to remain under the autonomous jurisdiction of the Weinstein House Commission and that the House Commission would permit any university organization, including Gay Student Liberation, to reserve space in the sub-cellar. They voted to support the sit-in and to keep the cops away.

Sylvia, Michael Morrissey, Martha Shelley, and the forty or fifty other people, including me, were told that we were now technically the guests of the students. As guests, we could remain in the downstairs area. "The only way they can stop you from coming in again is to make Weinstein a fortress against six hundred residents." Little did they know.

Integration flourished on Tuesday and Wednesday. Students came to the sub-basement and rapped. A consciousness-raising thing happened between gays and straights. Psyches were blooming and brotherhood and sisterhood were powerful.

Sylvia, who had been living out on the streets for a few days, now had a place to do his laundry. He and a new friend from the Coast named Bubbles found a matrons' bathroom in the basement where they washed their clothes. They showered there and dried themselves with paper towels. All of the transvestites threw their makeup together—Sylvia his mascara, Bubbles his foundation

114

base and powder—making for a communal makeup kitty. Some of the Radical Lesbians gave Sylvia hints on makeup, what to use, and how to use it. Sylvia discarded his male clothes and began dressing in drag.

He became friendly with a chubby, intelligent woman carpenter from GLF named Judy. "I never knew lesbians like you," said Sylvia. "The only lesbians I knew were street dykes. But you're really nice."

Judy said, "I feel the same way about you, Sylvia. I've never known any drag queens before."

"Transvestites," said Sylvia. "Transvestites."

Sylvia related well to the straight women students. The males tended to stay away. At one point Sylvia, in a little print dress with puffed sleeves and trousers, freshly shaven, was rapping "autonomy" with a freshman on the main floor of the dormitory. The discussion grew into a forum on homosexual rights. Sylvia handled himself with the aplomb of a Paul Cliffman.

Monday night Cary Yurman appeared. He had just resigned as city news reporter for *Gay,* so his visit to Weinstein was an unprofessional one. He wanted to see what was happening, and he stayed for the rest of the sit-in week.

Cary and I built up a friendship during those four days that appeared to be more than a friendship to some, including Paul Cliffman. What the some did not know is that Cary and I had too much in common to ever be lovers. Even so, we had our differences—Cary had strong opinions, mine were weak. I mostly parroted Paul and couldn't back up my arguments. I was very much a GAA man then, and Cary had already soured on the group.

We dined one evening in Chinatown and walked back to NYU through deserted Mulberry Street, past a neon-lighted Italian church, past parked trucks on litter-splattered streets. We talked about growing up in Chicago and Brooklyn and our first sexual encounters and thwarted dreams and future hopes, and I discovered that I respected this relative stranger more than anyone else I knew. Not only did I respect him, I liked him. And that doesn't happen often with me.

The third day of the sit-in, when good feelings were at a peak, Marty Robinson roared in wearing a lambda shirt and doing his "the mighty GAA is here to save you, whether you like it or not" routine. He berated the leader of the gay student group for not keeping GAA posted and lammed into me. "You should have called me. You should have kept in touch." I told him that he had two legs and could have come down any time, since he knew what was happening from the very start. I also told him that I was at Weinstein as an individual and not as a member of GAA. The scene with Marty took place in front of several people. It was heavy.

There was a group discussion later that evening about means of getting more people into the sub-basement. Some kids were feeling the shock of sleeping on pool tables and were talking about leaving for a good night at home. Feeling some guilt about Marty, I suggested that we get GAA to come down to support us. I was booed and told that GAA as an organization would force itself into a leadership position. Keep GAA away was the consensus. Far away.

Earlier that day the air-conditioner was turned off, and

instead of freezing the night away we sweltered. Very little sleep was had. We played charades and spin the bottle, sang, and bunny-hopped. Some of the students brought their mattresses and cots to the sub-basement and cohabited with us. Cary left for home to take care of his dog, Pluto, and I called my assistant at Random House asking her if she would cover me for just one more day. The sit-in would definitely be over tomorrow, I said. But it wasn't.

When tomorrow came, the Gay Student Liberation group conferred with school officials throughout the day. They were told that they could have gay dances, but that they could not invite the community. Did that mean that each of the ten members could invite one guest, thereby having a rousing dance for twenty in a sub-basement that resembled a Metro-Goldwyn-Mayer sound stage? Yes, it did. This was unacceptable to the sit-ins.

The student body and the squatters held a mass meeting that evening in the sub-basement cafeteria, far more boisterous and antagonistic than the resident meeting held three nights before. The net result was a contract drawn up by the House Commission supporting a "liberation" dance to be given at Weinstein on Friday, the following night. The students would only support the sit-ins until the end of the dance, after that we were on our own. It was rather a nebulous decision, since the problem of opening up Weinstein to the community became a side issue. The meeting was really about student power versus administrative power, with gay power as catalyst.

Administrative power had their day. At 2:30 Friday afternoon they ended the occupation. They called in the Tactical Patrol Force. All doors but one were chained, and the twenty-nine sit-ins, including Sylvia, were given ten seconds to get out, or else. The student House Commission dance contract of course was nullified.

I met Cary for dinner that evening. Cary had just been assigned to cover the story for the Los Angeles *Advocate,* and I had that day been asked to keep an eye out for a *Village Voice* article. Armed with notebooks and a tape recorder, we reached NYU at 7:30. All hell had broken loose. Barricades were set up at the corner of Eighth Street and University Place. A dozen patrol cars were parked on the street. Shouts of "Gay power" and "Power to the people" were heard, and we were greeted by Mike Morrissey with news of police violence.

It seems the cops had just busted three straight kids. One of the arresting officers fired into the air and aimed his gun at Sylvia and a small group who were protesting the arrests. The cop threatened to pull the trigger unless the crowd dispersed. So now the angry mob formed into a group march. Village residents, who three weeks previously had seen the fury of the homosexual community, witnessed another sight that night as Sylvia and Bubbles led a swarm of followers down Eighth Street to Sheridan Square and back to NYU. Little attention was paid to the police restrictions that we limit our march to the sidewalk, that we stroll in pairs of two. We took to the center of the street, holding hands, gays, straights, street people, transvestites, middle-class people, college kids, chanting, dancing, stomping, "Power to the people."

Where was GAA during all of this? Five or six individuals were out there demonstrating, but the membership at large preferred to stay away. Mike Morrissey said he phoned Marty Robinson that fateful night. "I called to 'keep him in touch,' " said Mike, "and to tell him that we were thrown out of the sub-cellar. I told him we were having a big demonstration and the cops were everywhere. Marty said he knew about it, that the whole thing had been planned by the radical elements of the Gay Liberation Front as a plot to confront the police. He said GAA didn't want to get involved. He was making 'tactical' decisions for the entire organization."

By midnight the demonstration broke up. Michael Morrissey tried to persuade Sylvia to go with him to Alternate U for the remaining hours of the night. (Alternate U is a "radical" school where GLF held dances and Gay Night classes. It's doors were open during much of the sit-in.) Sylvia was obstinate and refused to leave. It was as if he were defying the entire system that oppressed him. He said he'd sleep on the steps of Weinstein until they carried him away.

Late, late Saturday night, in bed with Paul, we talked briefly of the week's events. Paul said that he thought my being at Weinstein was fine, but that my motives weren't pure. He said I was responsible for keeping GAA away because of self-glorification. NYU was my baby, and the whole trip was an "I don't need them" deal. Paul was touching on some half-truths that hadn't crossed my mind, making me feel bad for something I knew was good. That evening I hated him for his logic and seriously thought of getting out, once and for all.

The following week was relatively quiet. There was sporadic marching and leafleting, and a new organization called Street Transvestites for Gay People was formed by Sylvia and the street people as a result of the NYU sit-in.

The organization, later to change its name to STAR (Street Transvestites Action Revolutionaries) issued its first leaflet:

> If you want Gay Power, then you're going to have to fight for it. And you're going to have to fight until you win. Once you start, you're not going to be able to stop, because if you do, you'll lose everything. If you want to fight for your rights, then fight till the end. All we fought for at Weinstein Hall was lost when we left upon the request of the pigs. Chalk one up for the pigs, and realize that the next demonstration is going to be harder because they now know that we scare easily. You people run if you want to, but we're tired of running. We intend to fight for our rights until we get them.

On Monday, October 5, picket lines formed at noon at Loeb Student Center. With a smaller than expected turn-out, approximately thirty people protested the intolerance of the university and its indifference to a list of demands presented by members of the gay community. The demands focused on three areas: community responsibility, educational responsibility, and the university's responsibility for Bellevue Hospital, which they help to staff.

Less than half of the protesters proceeded to Bellevue Hospital, where they held a silent demonstration. That evening a mass demonstration was called for at Loeb Center. It was hoped that gay people throughout the city, plus workers and students from other schools, would participate. The turnout again was disappointing.

A sound truck was set up. Impromptu speeches were given. ("We are everybody. We come from everywhere.

We know everything.") But by ten P.M. the demonstration had fizzled like a dead Bromo, and we were talking to ourselves again.

The following day I spoke to Chancellor Whiteman of NYU, the man who made the remark about "impressionable freshmen." I told him I was doing a story on the Weinstein affair for the *Voice* and asked if he'd answer the gay demands point by point.

"Maybe we're doing the best thing by replying to the public press," he said. "Like so many of the communications of today, it's hard to know who we ought to answer. The grievance form isn't addressed to anybody, nor is it signed.

"Let me say that the whole first series of demands [space for a twenty-four-hour gay community center, open enrollment and free tuition for gay people, open employment, facilities for child care centers] was really unrealistic and exaggerated almost to the point of creating a feeling that the homosexual community is not serious about those demands. We cannot, as part of the university, possibly turn over our property to non-university groups. If groups want to rent space, that's another matter entirely. Many groups need space which the university cannot provide legally or financially. To me those demands represent a deep sense of frustration in society rather than expectations that are positive. As for the Bellevue demands, all I can say is that I have the utmost confidence in our Bellevue medical staff. I cannot comment intelligently on shock treatment—I'm sure that it is used in certain instances. We've all read about those things. The demands on education are the most realistic and possible and probable ones and come closest to my concept of what a university ought to do. These demands are what we ought to tackle and get at. Let's create some sort of commission of knowledgeable people to examine what the teaching role, the social role of a university is, and how we can help through that line rather than through the unrealistic things proposed. I suggested to our students back in August that we form a committee of people that are knowledgeable and experienced in homosexuality, a committee of professionals in the field, sociologists, psychologists, psychiatrists, straight or gay. Let's get them together. Let's develop a teaching program.

"What happened here two weeks ago is part of this whole new concern for a new relationship of the university to the immediate surrounding community. It has been expressed by our students as well as outsiders. The old reference of responsibility and involvement meant students going out doing social work. Now it's open admission, providing facilities, issues that have nothing to do with gay people, but with the whole community.

"The big problem, unfortunately, here is money. The university is deeply in debt on an operational level, and we just do not have the capital."

On my way back to Random House, I bumped into Sylvia (after several visits to court, the case against Sylvia re his Carol Greitzer petitioning was dropped, and Sylvia had consequently abandoned the hustle of Forty-second Street for the bustle of Christopher). I told Sylvia about the Chancellor Whiteman interview. "Tell Whiteman the money problem is his problem," said Sylvia. "It isn't ours. Our problem is rights. And we're going to get our rights. And we'll be back at Weinstein to sit in for a year, if we have to. And we'll take over the rest of the campus. The university belongs to the people, and that means the gay people too. The issue has nothing to do with money. And he better believe it, the fuck."

Sylvia came to a GAA meeting a week or two after Weinstein to request a donation for STAR. Money was needed to rent quarters for the street people. Clothes were needed too. I proposed that GAA give STAR a hundred dollars from its treasury. Contributing money would start a precedent, was the decision. The motion was defeated. Instead Sylvia was told that he could leave a box at the front table for donations.

About this time, unbeknownst to the membership, Paul subliminally set up the groundwork for his presidential campaign. An orientation committee was proposed, its function to run "cluing-in" sessions for all new members, to act as hosts at all GAA functions, and to make recommendations to the executive committee on how to recruit new members. Paul, who had hitherto told all and sundry that he was most effective bereft of committee chairmanship, did an about-face and got orientation. The chairmanship served several purposes: he could verse new members on the political ways of the organization, his Rock of Gibraltar presence would make a never-to-be-forgotten introductory opener and a sure-to-be-remembered "vote" come election time. Plus, he could serve on the executive committee, a must for any presidential candidate, since the executive committee meetings were closed to all but committee chairmen.

Paul, let it be said, allowed GAAers on his committee to give orientation to the new people. I attended a session given by Michael Morrissey at an apartment on the Lower

East Side. Six GAA stalwarts were present, and five new people who had come for orienting.

We sit on the floor in a comfortably furnished double-parlor affair—all of us very serious. Michael talks about the GAA committees and their functions. "Social affairs," he says, "is mostly designed for dances. Fund-raising is, well, to raise funds for GAA. Orientation is this." The pupils listen in rapt attention, looking at their printed "What Is GAA" form, sneaking occasional glances at Michael's gorgeous face. "One of the things GAA does not do is officially endorse candidates," says Michael from his cushioned position in the corner. "If we did, it would seem we are making a tie with the candidates."

Smoke fills the room, cigar smoke. One of the neophytes has a coughing jag. "Please open the window," he says, and the host opens the window. Michael continues. "The Thursday night meetings are business meetings to keep us all in touch with what is happening. About seventy-five members show up every Thursday. You don't have to be a member to say what you think. The executive committee is the one place where committee chairmen can air their grievances. Most of our work is done in committee. If you decide to work in a certain committee, like the police power committee, you don't have to stay there. It's flexible."

Paul pipes in, "It is incumbent upon you as an activist to contribute to at least one committee. Of course, some committees are more efficient than others. When you go to the general meetings, you can just make a note of those that strike your interest. I want to point out a right you have as a voting member. We have a procedure of a vote of no confidence."

124

Paul then goes into the rules of parliamentary procedure. "Just know these rules. It's very basic. It's all you need."

"What kind of issues split the organization" asks a novice.

"Most of the split comes between right and left wing," answers Paul.

Michael touches on the summer raucousness with Natasha. "Some people in GAA are against transvestites," he says. "Some are against women. We've had a lot of women come to GAA. They're welcome, of course, but they see a vast sea of male faces and they're intimidated."

"What's the difference between GAA and GLF?"

"GLF in New York is both multi-issued and unstructured," answers Paul. "They believe that the U.S. government as it stands is in need of radical change. GLF believes in revolution. We, at GAA are into changing laws and working within the framework of the United States Constitution."

"Is there reasonably good feelings between the two groups?"

Michael replies, "There is little communication between the groups in New York. That's because there's no community council."

The host brings out tea and sponge cake. The cake plate goes around the room and winds up empty at Michael's feet. Two Siamese cats pounce on it.

"It's my personal hope that with the help of other groups we can become a national organization," says Paul. "We'll be holding GAA elections December seventeenth; the nominations are December tenth. You'll all be eligible to vote."

A new kid says, "If you don't see my membership within the next two weeks, it's not because you've done a bad job."

Paul, morose as an old buddha, sits there shaking his head. His communication is not by warmth, yet his strength is felt around the room. That overworked word "charisma"—sex appeal, a stillness and intelligence that create a presence that attracts the new ones, and bothers the old ones.

"What committees are there for people who aren't very political?" asks the coughing-jag newcomer.

Paul just sits there, shakes his head, and turns the floor back to Michael.

We slurped down Häagen-Dazs boysenberry sherbet that evening at our pre-sleep GAA talk. I was nude—my underpants were at the laundry—and horny—I hadn't had sex in eight days. I snuggled close to Paul but dared not start anything or say anything, fearful of rejection, embarassment, aftermaths more serious than immediate needs, wishing he'd sense I wanted sex with him, hoping he'd comply. He didn't. Instead, the nonsense of the moment of words. Words.

"How do you see yourself in terms of GAA?" I asked.

"I am a master architect," he said, rolling away, but touching my arm. "I see myself as a Machiavellian figure." Words. I didn't know exactly what Machiavellian was. I knew it had to do with politics and plotting and had an evil connotation, but I didn't give a damn that night, lying next to the man who told me he loved me, yet wouldn't love me, the man who knowingly had me in his hold.

And I wasn't able to break away on my own.

126

The following week I received an early morning phone call from Mel Shestack, the producer of a brand-new news telecast show scheduled to run Monday through Friday on WOR-TV. Shestack said the station wanted to do an in-depth study on gay liberation—one of their first special coverage spots. Could he and his camera crew come over in an hour? Of course, I said, downing a cup of black coffee.

I woke up the gay activist I spent the night with, shaved and showered, and shortly thereafter placed myself on the living room couch for a face-to-face interview with Bill Ryan, the sincere-as-hell WOR anchorman.

The following morning Mel Shestack phoned again. The film came out fine, he said. Could WOR cover one of our meetings? Shestack also asked if his crew could follow me to work with their cameras. The film he had shot had taken a direction—it had evolved into a salute to the human aspect of an uncloseted homosexual in Manhattan. ("Sometimes when the weather is nice, Mr. Bell walks to work. There is nothing to distinguish him from other New Yorkers, except that he is an admitted homosexual.")

They decided to stretch the segment to a three-part series. The program was shown November 17, 18, and 19. The first part was mostly a question and answer session on the parlor couch, interwoven with lots of walking. Very Antonioni. The second part used my voice-over: "Gay liberation covers a complete spectrum, kids of sixteen and seventeen, high school kids, men in their late sixties. As far as religion, we run the gamut—Protestant, Jewish,

Catholic, everything. Minority groups—we have them. Homosexuality is a minority group in itself. Unfortunately, there are many homosexuals who are middle class aspiring to upper middle class. They are afraid of getting themselves involved. They're trying to 'pass'—we hope to eventually reach them. These people are afraid of the homosexual who is in the movement. They are afraid of what 'popularizing' homosexuality may do to them." While I talked, the camera panned over a GAA meeting. It took in individual faces, many beautiful, many members of those minority groups I described. It was a splendid job of editing and cutting. The third segment ended with Bill Ryan asking the ridiculous question "Will you ever be happy?" I replied that when my work goes good and my love life is good, I'm attuned to the world. Being attuned is never constant with me, therefore I can never be completely happy. Can you?

The program ratings went up five points that week, making WOR attuned to the world and happy. Gay is good box office.

Jean Ennis died October 16. My boss lady, respected and loved by everyone, was suddenly no more. Her death was a shock to those who knew her and saw her each day. It happened suddenly.

Jean hosted two parties the week of her death. The first was a mammoth affair at the New York Times building honoring *The Great Song Hits of the Sixties*. Jean that day wore a maxi-skirt for the first time and was girlishly apprehensive about her appearance. She looked swell, but needed assuring.

The day before her death Jean gave a bash for the art and literary worlds to celebrate publication of *Facing East* by James Michener and Jack Levine. Jean looked haggard that day. She said she was catching a cold. On Friday she left the office at five, unusual for her. She said good night, glad that the hectic week was over.

Monday there was no word from Jean. She had scheduled a publication-day luncheon with an author, who unsuccessfully tried to reach her at home. Shortly after noon Jean's secretary taxied to her apartment. She couldn't get in. The police were called. They busted the front door. Jean was found on the kitchen floor, dead three days of a heart attack.

Jean was without immediate family. Her next of kin was a cousin. It was up to her co-workers to arrange the funeral service.

Bennett Cerf, Rabbi Joseph Gefflen, and authors Elie Wiesel and Herbert Tarr delivered eulogies. Wiesel, in a voice vibrating with emotion, said that Jean knew everybody and was known by everybody. She was a friend to us all and asked for nothing. Why, at the end, was nobody there? Each of us is to blame for the shame that Jean Ennis died alone.

A few days after Jean's death I gave Random House three weeks' notice and spent little time at my job after that.

I couldn't pass Jean's empty office without a million thoughts about a million things entering my head. Instead, I threw myself into a surge of outside GAA activity that took place during the last week of October: a Lindsay zap, a zap at *Harper's Magazine,* an "almost" zap of the

Dick Cavett Show, another visit to Criminal Court with the Rockefeller Five (actually Rockefeller Four—Phil Raia had left town), a press conference, and leafleting like crazy for the Democratic and Republican candidates in New York who had spoken out on homosexual rights.

The Lindsay zap took place at a preview performance of the Danny Kaye play, *Two by Two.* Society turned out for the occasion and *The New York Times* covered the gala on its society page. The *Times* noted that a dozen men from a gay liberation group shouted at the Lindsays, "Homosexuals need your help," five times in unison, then, "End police harassment, end police harassment."

The mayor apparently looked straight ahead, and the dowager lady hostessing the benefit said, "My God, they came right at us. Anything could have happened. I mean, where were the police?"

What the *Times* failed to report was that Mary Lindsay scratched and kicked at the GAA contingent. Paul got it in the shins, and Eben Clark got hit in the chest twice.

According to Eben, "The confrontation lasted ten minutes. The show was in the lobby, not in the theater. Many ticket holders pushed forward, creating a show themselves. And strangely, many chanted with us.

"After Mrs. Lindsay had finished her karate chops, the mayor turned and pointed an accusing finger at her, like he let go of his cool and gave it to her. I don't think Mrs. Lindsay was frightened by the zap. She was angry. She was there with her friends, and we had the nerve to bring up a John Lindsay political issue during a social affair."

GAA's fifth Lindsay zap did not result in a statement from the mayor, nor did it win any new friends for GAA. It did, however, prompt Jean De Vente, the softball team captain, to recommend that we get ourselves a class in self defense "for just such emergencies in the future."

As usual, a few faithfuls appeared at Criminal Court to support the Rockefeller Five. If tried, the case would come before a three-man tribunal. If convicted, the Five would face a maximum three-month sentence.

The case was postponed on a legal technicality called recognizance. This meant that the defendants were free to go about their business for the next four months. Barring complications, the Republican State Committee would probably drop charges. Pressing charges a week before elections would be a political embarrassment. "It's called copping out," said Jim Owles, who is all for political embarrassment. Four months later, sure enough, charges were dropped.

We dropped a pretty bombshell that week on *Harper's Magazine*. The September 1970 issue contained a cover story by Joseph Epstein titled "Homo/Hetero: The Struggle for Sexual Identity." In it, Epstein wrote that homosexuality is an anathema "to be wished off the face of this earth," that homosexuals are different from the rest of us, that we are cursed with no clear cause to our rationality (oops!). He concluded with a statement that one can tolerate homosexuality, but accepting it is another thing altogether. Nothing could ever make him sadder than if any of his four children were to become homosexuals (murderers O.K., but not gay!), because then they'd be "condemned to a state of permanent niggerdom among men, their lives, whatever adjustment they might make to their condition, to be lived out as part of the pain of the earth."

We had a lulu this time, and Peter Fisher, a political-theory major at Columbia, young, bright, somewhat conservative, musically talented, and out full blast, was chosen to head the *Harper's* committee. It was a committee I was interested in. I attended meetings at Pete's basement apartment to plan the sit-in strategy.

The initial strategy was to submit four articles to *Harper's* written by GAA members. Each was quite good, each quite different from the other. None of the articles directly attacked Epstein's piece; they stood on their own. As quickly as the articles were submitted, they were rejected. *Harper's* also rejected the idea of commissioning an unprejudiced article from another source for publication.

Having gone the acceptable route, the committee then planned to move into the *Harper's* office. How to do it? A party—a breakfast party celebrating homosexuality, a sort of teach-in, be-in. Have a cup of coffee and a prune danish and meet and rap with a living, breathing homosexual. Separate Epstein's myth from reality. Breakfast at *Harper's*. The committee printed an excellent pamphlet accusing *Harper's* of irresponsible publishing (to clearly associate itself with this type of opinion *Harper's* is blatantly discriminatory toward homosexuals), exploitation (tasteless photos on the cover and within the magazine are demeaning to homosexuals), manipulative pseudo liberalism, and cheap and unacceptable tokenism (printing a series of letters in its November issue—a wholly inadequate way of redressing the imbalances of a prejudicial feature story).

We held a rehearsal meeting at my apartment the night before the sit-in. Fifty-five people attended, including Merle Miller, author and former managing editor of *Harper's,* and contributing writer to *The New York Times Magazine.* Miller drafted a letter sanctioning the protest; he could not believe that *Harper's* would print such an attack on any other minority group in America. As it happened, the *Harper's* action turned out to be political, consciousness-raising, and fun, and it went over with a bang for everyone—from Marty Robinson and Jim Owles to the kids with shining eyes visiting their first publishing house.

Early the zap morning a group met at a corner adjacent to the Harper building. Our plan was to invade early, set up the coffee machine, make ourselves comfortable before the biggies got in. Two of our members were posted outside the building to hand out pamphlets to passers-by. Two more took to the corridors of Harper & Row, Publishers, where they distributed leaflets until they were chased out of the building by an office manager.

At nine A.M. forty of us got off the elevators at the eighteenth floor and crashed. "Hello, I'm a homosexual," said Eben Clark to the receptionist-switchboard operator. "I'm here to show you what homosexuals are really like." And that he did, and we did. We took over.

We held informal discussions in the board room, in private offices, in the production department, in the reception area. A couple of *Harper's* employees conceded that the article was way off base. A middle-aged woman at the switchboard admitted that this was her first encounter with homosexuals and she was having a perfectly wonderful day. Our pamphleting in the street resulted in an on-slaught of lunchtime visitors. They roamed the Harper offices and responded graciously to "Hi, my name is . . . I'm a homosexual. Would you like a cup of coffee? Cream and sugar? Pamphlet?"

Midge Decter, editor of the infamous Epstein slip, argued in favor of the article. "It is serious and honest and was misread," she said. "It does not reinforce anti-homosexual prejudice. The question of changing the minds and hearts of men is a complicated one that does not yield to political demands. It works in other ways."

To which Paul, in top finger-pointing, voice-blasting form, responded, "You knew that his article would contribute to the suffering of homosexuals. You knew that. And if you didn't know that, you're inexcusably naïve. If you know that those views contribute to the oppression of homosexuals, then damn you for publishing that article. We have a right to come here and hold you politically and morally responsible for it. You are a bigot and you are to be held responsible for that moral and political act." Midge Decter left at noon for lunch and did not return.

During the afternoon, Pete Fisher brought out his guitar. He plopped himself on the floor near the switchboard, and, with a little help from his GAA friends, strummed and sang his original composition "The Time Is Now."

> Sometimes it's hard to take a stand,
> It's hard to say what must be said.
> Sometimes the writing's on the wall,
> And it's waiting to be read.
> The time is now, brother, the time is now.
> The time is now, sister, the time is now.

We were joined by Harper employees and by visitors who had wandered in. Our voices were heard throughout the building. We had liberated *Harper's Magazine,* and we all felt the best that we had felt as GAA "taking a stand" in a long, long time.

Instead of heading toward the nearest bar to celebrate, we took the subway to ABC-TV and the *Dick Cavett Show.* The Cavett zap had been planned a month before. We had written away for tickets and received a combined total of fifty.

Cavett, on his national television talk show, had hosted a couple of late spring, early summer guests—comedian Mort Sahl was one of them—whose anti-homosexual remarks were both inopportune and offensive. We requested rebuttal time.

In late spring Marty Robinson and Jim Owles were interviewed by Cavett's pretty program director. She didn't want Jim. She had seen him on an ABC interview and was unimpressed by his appearance. Marty she had reservations about, but she said he might work.

The day following Mort Sahl's appearance I made an angry phone call from a telephone booth opposite the Criminal Court building, where we had come to support the Rockefeller Five. Marty stood outside the booth making signs.

"We want on," I said. "Equal time."

The program director suggested I come down with Marty—she'd talk to him again. She also asked me to bring one of our female members.

A week later we appeared. Without Jim, it seems, Marty was less nervous energy and more articulate. Jean De

Vente, our female representative, was natural and honest, but unfortunately she was not the image the program director wanted.

"I'll get back to you," she said. She didn't.

Six or seven weeks of frantic calling by me and passing the buck by them resulted in nilch. Marty wrote a letter of protest to John Gilroy, the Cavett director. Nothing came of that. So GAA set up a Cavett zap committee. Out of that came the writing for tickets for October 27, day of the proposed disruption.

On zap day we infiltrated the line of out-of-town tourists. Fresh from our *Harper's* victory, there was a look of maniacal glee glittering from many eyes. Somehow, word got out to the Cavett staff that we were there. One of the braid-suited ushers paraded the line, remarking that Cavett management was ready to negotiate a GAA appearance. Would a few representatives follow him? The Cavett people would discuss a definite time slot.

So they set a date for November 27, the Friday after Thanksgiving. Cavett would have two members of our choosing as his guests. Satisfied, we called off the zap, saving the show a considerable amount of money. We were prepared to interrupt the program with whistles. Since the program was taped four hours prior to air time, there'd be time to cut out the zap, but retaping extra footage is costly.

The GAA Cavett committee was a farce. I made a motion at a general meeting that the membership select the GAA Cavett guest stars. Several people with something to gain by committee selectivity spoke against the motion, and it was voted down. Instead, a committee meeting was held at Marty Robinson's apartment. Those who attended would select five finalists, two of whom in turn would be chosen by the Cavett people for the program. Competitiveness was rampant. Jim Owles, Eben Clark, and Paul Cliffman, the GAA presidential candidates, were at the meeting. In the final balloting they, plus Pete Fisher and Marty Robinson, won out. Because Marty Robinson was more or less preselected by the Cavett program people, because Jim Owles was not wanted by them, and because Pete Fisher does not come across on TV, the Cavett selection was narrowed down to Eben Clark and Paul Cliffman. Paul got it. He and Marty Robinson would appear with Phyllis Diller, James Earl Jones, and Nora Ephron on the *Dick Cavett Show* on November 27. For the first time GAA goes national.

"Leafleting is fun," said Marc Rubin, pitching for leafleteers at a GAA meeting. Marc is a sweet guy, very sincere, liked by almost everyone. He got his leafleteers.

Marc and his election committee worked out a bang-up pre-election campaign. They systematically questioned all the Democratic and Republican candidates running in New York City concerning their positions on homosexual rights. Sample questions: Would you favor repealing the New York sodomy and solicitation laws? Would you favor extending existing fair employment laws to homosexuals? Would you favor ending income tax discrimination against single persons?

It worked. For the first time in New York a number of major candidates put themselves on the line and spoke out on the gay issue. Some candidates needed prodding, and got it. For Arthur Goldberg, Democratic gubernatorial candidate, it didn't come easy. Back in June, Goldberg was zapped by GAA at a rally on Broadway and Eighty-sixth Street. Loudly and vigorously he was questioned on homosexual issues. His car was surrounded. "I have more important matters to talk about," he said, visibly shaken, and for the first time faced with the force of the new homosexual.

Two weeks prior to the election, however, Goldberg

issued a statement. It was to be released on October 25 (state elections were November 3), and it read:

> Homosexuality has been treated by our society as a criminal problem, with harsh and discriminatory laws, for too long. I believe that issues concerning consenting relations between adults in private are mishandled when they are dealt with adversely in the legal area. Questions of fair employment, bonding, police harassment and other related matters should not be answered negatively for a man or woman just because his or her private life involves homosexuality. Present laws and present attitudes are wrong. The law must change and social attitudes must change. I will work to these ends if I am elected.

It was the first time that a gubernatorial candidate had come out openly in favor of homosexual rights.

Rockefeller continued to avoid the gay issue like the bubonic plague. A confrontation between Marty Robinson and Rockefeller at the Piccadilly Hotel resulted in nothing. And the publicized sit-in at Republican State Committee headquarters didn't make a dent. Rocky, like Gibraltar, remained silent.

On the senatorial level both Charles Goodell (Republican) and Richard Ottinger (Democrat) came out with positive statements. I cornered Ottinger at the New Democratic Coalition convention in August. "All of the speakers are talking about helping minority groups—blacks, chicanos, women," I said, "yet not a single person has said anything about homosexuals. Would you?"

Ottinger answered, "I have no problem with that at all. I'll put something out, or make it part of a platform, if I have a platform."

The something that Ottinger put out was a good, lengthy statement endorsing the rights of homosexuals to live their lives free of political, social, and economic harassment and discrimination. Ottinger also sent one of his speakers to our Thursday meeting. The speaker, alas, was a poor substitute for his boss. He failed miserably in the question and answer period.

Charles Goodell's first statement tended to encompass all minority groups. Marc Rubin insisted that the Goodell camp be specific on homosexuality, and Goodell came back with "Constitutional principles are today clearly being abridged and denied in reference to homosexuals, and I therefore support efforts to secure their basic rights under the Constitution."

More than fifty statements were received from the two hundred or so sent out. Some responses were off the beaten track. Most were favorable. Marc and his committee graded the answers on a percentage basis and drew up a leaflet report card. The leaflet, which could be taken into the voting booth for referral, listed all of the Manhattan, Brooklyn, Queens, and Bronx candidates who responded favorably to the nine-point questionnaire. Another leaflet, headed "Your Candidates Speak Out on Homosexual Rights," ended with "Although GAA does not endorse candidates, it is clear that the political cowardice and arrogance of those candidates who have refused a response, and political awareness of those who have responded, should be taken into account on Election Day."

Of course Rockefeller, arrogance and all, was to win the election from Goldberg; and Goodell and Ottinger, with all of their political awareness, were to lose the election to Jim Buckley, a conservative who refused to "speak out."

Still, several politicians pushing gay rights did well at the polls. Particularly happy was the shoo-in of Bella Abzug. We were hoping it would work for Bella the moment she opened her mouth at our GAA meeting back in April. Bella had won herself a reputation as the Ethel Merman of politics. She was loud, brassy, and good-intentioned. We rooted for her and sang hosannas when she beat Barry Farber, the Republican candidate.

GAA is mostly a Village-based organization. Eben Clark and Marc Rubin, however, took it upon themselves to campaign heavily for Tony Olivieri, a young Democrat running for State Assembly on the Upper East Side. The Upper East Side is a location noted for its surplus of closet homosexuals. Closeted or flagrant, we were determined to inform all of our poll-taking: our campaigning was pure open chutzpah. A brigade of pamphleteers was sent to Bloomingdale's, heavy with Saturday shoppers, and Third Avenue, heavy with weekend cruisers. Looks of "How did you know?" crossed the faces of the closet brigade, upset that passing strangers might take them for one of "those." Many of "those" shied away from the blatant pamphleteers or destroyed the questionnaire in a rush. The sad truth of conditioning. Still, the uptown campaign was worthwhile. We did reach a number of homosexuals curious enough to read and go by the results of the questionnaire, and heterosexuals too, were impressed by the liberalness of the candidates' endorsements.

A special pamphlet was distributed in Tony Olivieri's district on election day. The pamphlet emphasized Olivieri's 100 per cent position endorsement, as well as the responses of five other candidates in that area.

Olivieri won the election by approximately 700 votes.

He was gentleman enough to acknowledge the fact that "GAA's consistent leafleting and posting of signs clearly had an impact." Olivieri further said that "after GAA had handed out their leaflets a substantial number of people stopped me to express their outrage at the fact my opponent had refused to answer the GAA questionnaire; similarly, they congratulated me on my stand." It was the first time that a Democratic State Assemblyman had been elected to office in the Sixty-sixth District in fifty-four years.

Pamphleting indeed was the major form of communication during the election. More than 50,000 were distributed in two weeks.

There was little press coverage of the "homosexual rights" issue. Marc and I visited *The New York Times* news desk with Goldberg's statement the Saturday it was scheduled for release. We talked to a reporter; Marc gave him a rundown of the operation of his election committee and handed him the Ottinger and Goodell statements as well. The reporter claimed that, barring a crisis in the Far East, the story would make the front page of Monday's edition. Monday came and not a word in print. Several phone calls and a couple of visits were made to the *Times* and it was learned that somewhere high above, the story was squashed. We raised a stink to the skies. On Wednesday a tiny box appeared buried deep in the paper: "Three Candidates Support Rights of Homosexuals."

The New York *Post* didn't pick up on the story at all. The AP wire services covered it, and the *Voice* ran an article that I wrote. My article, too, was judiciously cut.

The unofficial news blackout prompted the formation of

a *New York Times* committee. (Media, beware!) Marty Robinson relinquished his position as chairman of the political projects committee (someone seconded his resignation) to chair the *Times* committee. The committee's tactics are very clever. Marty Robinson is very clever.

Toward the end of the week that was, we called a press conference. Our news committee set the thing up, taking care of calls and working like mad on press releases.

We held the conference at an artist's loft on West Twenty-second Street. Although fifty calls were made, six people attended as press representatives, and three of those six were free-lance writers. The others represented *Coronet* magazine, ABC Radio, and *Women's Wear Daily*. Our gay panel and our GAA audience outnumbered our guests three to one. The GAA contingent included Jim Owles, Eben Clark, and a representative of the elections committee. Also on the panel were Tony Olivieri, Eldon Clingan—the City Council minority leader who was working on the passage of a homosexual fair employment bill —plus a representative of the New Democratic Coalition. I chaired the conference.

The thrust of Jim Owles's speech was on the news media blackout. Our elections committee representative went into the specifics of the politicians' statements on gay rights. He was articulate, as was Jim, but the star of the conference was Eben Clark. Completely off the cuff, Eben delivered a short statement on Mayor Lindsay's refusal to meet with the homosexual community. He was neither negative toward Lindsay, nor did he come down heavy on oppression. Instead he explained that Lindsay had an apparently good attitude toward homosexuals, but had neither spoken out nor put anything into writing, and therefore had laid no groundwork. Eben then elaborated on the press blackout, particularly in terms of *The New York Times*. He pointed out that today's turnout was a good example of media's attitude toward homosexuals. The press showed up for a gay "shock" story, they covered violence and riots, but refused to print news of a healthier nature. This was particularly disturbing to a group working within the system. Eben continued that the press encouraged myths about homosexuals by refusing to print news contrary to the American Image, and he recalled the telephone operator at the Harper reception room who, as we were leaving for the day, thanked us and pointed out to the television cameramen that we were her "friends." This woman hitherto thought that homosexuals were "different" from other human beings—that we came from out of the sky or from the sea. We were, in fact, no different from anyone else, she said, maybe nicer, and she would miss us the next day. Eben said that Mel Shestack of WOR-TV had asked him to specify what homosexuals had contributed to society. He retorted he had no idea since only bad things were attributed to homosexuals. Once a homosexual accomplished something of merit, he put on the mask of a heterosexual, "for acceptance."

As Eben spoke, he confirmed my belief: Eben was a man who represented the political as well as the human side of liberation, a man who could articulate his views in a straightforward, compassionate way. Eben neither lectured nor pontificated. He clarified. I would support Eben Clark for the presidency of GAA.

When the new committee structure was formed following the pleasure committee blowup in July, the executive committee voted among themselves to keep their meetings closed to the general membership; the meetings would be attended only by the elected officers and committee chairmen. Jim Owles mentioned the closed meetings as a *fait accompli.* There was no discussion, nor was the issue voted upon by the membership at large. If one had a matter of importance to present to the executive committee, he could come to the closed meeting, speak, then, literally, get out.

I visited the executive committee to propose that we hold a news conference following the Harper zap.

I brought up the point then that the membership was not given an opportunity to discuss the feasibility of closed executive committee sessions. I also suggested that the name "executive committee" be changed to "coordinating committee." There had grown an ever-widening gap between the membership and the so-called power structure. By having the membership come to those meetings, by ridding ourselves of the affronting word "executive," I felt there'd be less of a gap.

A vote was taken among the "executives" at the meeting that evening. Again it was decided to keep the meetings closed.

At the general membership meeting that followed, a couple of nasty issues developed. Sylvia requested that we lend STAR our stereo equipment for their first dance. As was the fashion, in the past month or two Sylvia was treated like a freak show. Sylvia's mere presence set members to shit in their pants. "When we started GAA, we hadn't a thing either," said one of our less liberated souls. "Why should we loan out our equipment? We're not in the rental business—there are people who are." Jim Owles also made a few cutting remarks about being pressured by STAR, and he was opposed to our lending the equipment. At the same meeting we allocated thirty-five dollars from our treasury to be spent on Christmas cards. The card was to have a big lambda on the front; the inside message, "Have a GAA Christmas."

I opened my mouth good and loud about the gross commercialization of our organization. I talked in terms of priorities. Why no money for the street people, yet we put dollars into cheap company salesmanship?

Jim Owles said, "Bell, why don't you take a flying fuck."

Without the use of proper parliamentary procedure, I grabbed the microphone. "I have a few words to say," I said, "and I'm going to say them." My words were that GAA was going in the wrong direction, that we were resembling big business as its worst, and that we had better get back in the right direction, quick. When we were out doing things, we were marvelous, but when we sat and talked about how marvelous we were, we were little people. I then talked about the fact that the executive committee meetings were closed and that the decision had not gone through the membership at large. I proposed that we take a vote on whether or not the meetings should be open to the general membership. Pete Fisher stood up and suggested that this point be brought up in the new committee on committees. Pete had just been given this chairmanship, a pat on the back for his good Harper work.

Several street people and one or two of the silent but grumbling minority supported my spiel. Those who thought GAA could do no wrong looked uncomfortable and talked in whispers.

At any rate, opening the executive committee meeting to the membership was discussed and approved at the first committee on committees meetings. Those same people, including Paul, who among themselves voted against opening the executive meetings to general membership did an about-face now that the matter was out in the open. They unanimously voted for opening the committee to the membership at large.

Cary Yurman was keeping away from our meetings. He was fed up with GAA—it had developed into the Mattachine Society of the 1970s, he said. Cary wasn't working. He had stopped writing. His money was low, and he was often depressed. We'd go to old movies—*The Philadelphia Story* and *Wife Versus Secretary*—dine on bacon sandwiches, and walk Pluto around the block. The things I did with Cary were the things that I enjoyed doing, and didn't do with Paul. Everything but sex. I did that with neither.

Sex came on a catch-as-catch-can basis. I had inhibitions about talking to people that I liked at our Thursday meetings. Paul was always there, and it was a standard rule that we leave with each other. Once a member called telling me he had read a movie review I did on *Sherlock Holmes* and asked if he could come over. He did, and we smoked and watched Eddie Cantor in *Roman Scandals* on television, and screwed. It wasn't satisfying.

Paul and I saw each other two or three times a week. When we met we talked GAA. Running monologues by him. Verbal algebra. If I did this, he'd say, then so and so would happen and such and such would follow. The GAA elections were close and Paul's presidency campaign had taken over his life. He was plotting his campaign carefully, too carefully. He honestly believed he'd win.

I didn't like what he was doing and accused him of manipulating people. He answered that he told no lies. "You can be honest as hell," I said, "and still manipulate. You drop truths discriminately, and hold back truths just as discriminately."

To that he replied two words.

Unfortunately, Paul's surge for power happened at a time when I had just left my job. I hadn't adjusted to a new routine yet. I was on my own for the first time and felt at sea. There was no encouragement from Paul. My self-esteem, moderate to low at best, reached a new low. I would perk up after sex with a trick picked up in Central Park, but would fall on my face immediately thereafter. The "types" I selected as bedmates during that period were "types" I wouldn't wish on my worst enemy. I was my worst enemy.

I must have been terribly frightened at the prospect of being left out in the cold. Paul's manipulatings became bigger than life, and I made much out of his total neglect of me. I felt very much alone.

Morty Manford and Paul and I stopped for coffee after one of our Thursday meetings. Morty said that the East Coast was minus a big charismatic gay figure. Paul had the potential. Morty offered to work like fury on Paul's campaign. "Get yourself seen and heard by the new members who haven't heard the glowing Cliffman speeches of the early days of GAA. Speak out on the floor. Speak out loudly on the issues that move you."

Morty's spiel sent illusions of sugarplums to Paul's

head. When we got home that evening, Paul was antagonistic and hostile. I couldn't take it. I told him I was going to support Eben Clark for the presidency.

"That's all right," he said. "Eben won't win."

His self-assuredness took me further away. "I'm supporting him anyway."

O<small>N</small> N<small>OVEMBER</small> 13, my last day at Random House, the publicity department gave me a going-away party. Four men attended, and forty women.

Several of the guests commented on the WOR television shot. Champagne flowed. I left the party high, down, and blue.

That night I had a dream. I was waiting for a self-service elevator at the Random House building. When it stopped, I found Phyllis Cerf, alone and glamorous. I entered the elevator and talked to her, but Mrs. Cerf refused to answer me. The elevator slowly descended to Bennett Cerf's office. Mrs. Cerf introduced me as "my good friend" to her husband. She said she didn't talk to me on the elevator because her mind was elsewhere. She didn't feel my small talk justified an answer.

An interview with Jim Owles appeared in the New York *Post* on November 5. Headlined "Gay Bill of Rights Makes Progress," the article by Lindsy Van Gelder began:

New York Homosexuals—who last year came out of hiding and onto the barricades—are turning their efforts to establishment politics. Among the developments: two prestigious City Councilmen are discussing the introduction of a bill barring job discrimination against homosexuals. . . .

And the City Human Rights Commission, while not legally empowered to represent the gay community, is cooperating with City Council members and others interested in the problem.

. . . At present, GAA is stockpiling affidavits of anti-gay job discrimination. Jim Owles believes the proposed fair employment bill is a priority because "people in the gay community can't fight for our other rights if they think they're going to lose their jobs." In the past, GAA has used sit-ins, demonstrations, disruptions of meetings and verbal harassment to make its points. "And we'll do all that to the City Council members who don't go along," Owles said.

Jim's public threat came as a rotten surprise to Richie Aunateau and his fair employment committee. At our general meeting held the day on which the article appeared, the fair employment committee members accused Jim of issuing a statement that hurt the work that they were doing and which might conceivably nullify their dealings with the Human Rights Commission. Jim's *Post* statement was issued without consulting Richie or anyone on the committee, they said.

The following week, Richie Aunateau did not attend the general Thursday night meeting. He sent in a letter of resignation. It was read to the membership, along with a statement by the members of his committee. The gist of the statement was that the negotiating authority of the fair employment committee had been undermined, in fact, kidnaped away by Owles. The committee could not function under those circumstances.

After the statement was read, Jim Owles bounced back with, "I had to step in. There's been a lot of soft talk from

Richie and the fair employment committee on getting the employment bill passed. If I'm to be a spokesman for GAA, I have to speak when there is a vacuum."

Whether or not Jim was wise to put his vacuum to a clean rug was debated and argued by the membership and ultimately referred to the executive committee for "ironing out."

The executive committee meeting takes place a few days later at Jim Owles's apartment. Marty, with a new short hair style, special for the Dick Cavett Show, is perched atop a peacock-blue desk, a brick fireplace in back of him. He sits with his legs crossed in a Buddha position, a couple of feet higher than the rest of the members, who are spread out on couches and on the floor of the small living room. I'm on a chair between Paul and Jim Owles.

Jim begins, "Let's discuss the dispute involving the fair employment committee." Marty, in a let's-all-be-buddies mood, says something about better communication. Richie replies, "I'm not here to discuss this organization's communication problems. I'm here to answer personal charges directed at me." He reads a statement chastising Owles for circumventing the work of his committee.

"Owles never attended a meeting of my committee and Robinson attended only one, where he expressed no disagreement with what we were doing."

Richie goes into detail about the meetings he had set up with the Human Rights Commission, and how Owles and Robinson went ahead and set up meetings of their own, undermining his work, and possibly negating his committee's strategy. He ends with "this thoughtless style of diplomacy is characteristic of certain spokesmen for GAA and is one of the reasons why I can no longer represent them publicly as a committee chairman."

Richie folds his statement in two. His dark eyes look down to the floor. His face is scarlet. "If I was at fault for negotiating on a point that's contrary to Marty's and to your own, you should have brought your gripe to our committee meeting instead of making threats in the pages of the *Post*."

Marty Robinson, arbitrator, pipes in: "Jim did not intend a personality attack on you, Richie. Jim felt that certain things were not accurately done. There was no political attempt on his part or mine to subvert your committee."

"Let Jim speak for himself," says Richie.

"I wasn't interested in going to your committee and downgrading you," says Jim. "The Human Rights Commission did a backtrack."

"How would you know?" asks Richie. "That's not true."

Jim starts to open his mouth, Marty cuts in. "Jim was worried about the way you were representing GAA politics. When it comes to hard points you weren't tough enough. Jim was defending the essence of the organization."

"In the pages of the *Post*?" asks Richie. "The only threat to the essence of the organization is you. I was working out a strategy for hearings. If you didn't agree with that strategy, you and Jim could have come to our committee meetings or just called me to voice your complaints. No one had the right to make the decision that you arbitrarily made while we were still in the process of negotiating."

Electricity in the air. Marty is stalking the room, back and forth, back and forth. He halts in front of Jim. All eyes are on Jim's face. "The Human Rights Commission sent up a trial balloon and you should have shot it down. I shot it down for you."

Eben Clark, from his corner, says, "There is a bad thing happening here. I think you, Jim, and you, Marty, have done bad things. If you didn't like the direction of the fair employment committee, you could have asked the chairman to beef up that committee or step down without taking things into your own hands."

I ask Richie to reconsider his resignation. He says he will. The meeting breaks.

Richie did reconsider and decided to stay. I attended the fair employment committee meeting held a few days after the shootout at the executive committee. Jim Owles attended, too. (The elections were close, and Jim and Paul were now beginning to attend meetings of the committees where they weren't loved, to campaign for love—and votes. If they themselves couldn't attend, they'd send one of their supporters.)

Again, hearings of the Human Rights Commission were discussed—whether the hearings should be opened or closed. Was the commission aware of gay liberation as a political force? Richie seemed to think so. If not, they would be—his committee had a dozen cases of job discrimination in various areas of business, and all of the claimants were willing to testify.

The meeting lasted a couple of hours. Each committee member was assigned a job by Richie, and given a check-in phone number for during-the-week communication.

I left the meeting with Jim and had coffee with him. He was in a zippy mood, having seemingly reestablished himself with the fair employment committee. We talked about sex and the joys and frustrations of living in New York, and Jim consciously avoided all references to GAA politics and the elections. Once again, I was reminded that Jim is another trip, a more pleasant trip, away from the Sturm und Drang of Marty Robinson and civil libertarian politics.

Paul and I went to STAR's first dance at Alternate U. Though Paul seemed out of it, I had a marvelous time dancing with many of the people that I had slept in with at NYU.

The dance floor was decorated with little Christmas bulbs that flashed on and off, and little spangled balls in neckless arrangements. Someone had scribbled, "If experience is destroyed, behavior will be destroyed," on a yellow wall. The dancers were behaving in an experienced, undestructive manner. They shook their asses and stomped and strutted. The costumes were fantastic: an all black body-form jump suit with bottoms disappearing into red boots. Bob Kohler of GLF wore a white T-shirt with thousands of beads and a beautiful Indian sash dripping from his left hip. Sylvia dressed in pants and blouse. He was at the door collecting donations. Every now and then he'd hand a wad of green to Bob Kohler, which Bob would deposit in a safe. Sylvia was tired and irritable. He claimed he hadn't slept in days. His underarms gave forth an odor that permeated the air around him.

Shortly after midnight Sylvia stopped the music and made a speech: "This dance is for the people of the streets who are part of our gay community. Let's give them a better chance than I had when I came out. I don't know if any of you ever lived out on the streets. I do. So do many of the transvestites who make up STAR. We are asking you for money tonight. Winter is coming and we need money for clothes and rent. Please dig into your pockets and help STAR."

Paul asked Sylvia that evening if he would make his presidential nominating speech. Paul was aware that the membership of GAA was now mostly moderate conservative. Most of the conservatives, he felt, would vote for Jim Owles. Paul was hoping to get the radical vote, the college vote, and the vote of many of the old members. He realized that Sylvia's nominating speech would mean the support of the street people and the radicals. And Sylvia, that spaced-out night, agreed to nominate Paul.

Dıck Cavett is a teensy fellow. He's got high cheekbones and a defined chin and definite opinions and a way of drawing unspeakable speeches from the guest stars that visit his nighttime ninety-minute talk show.

I had been to Cavett's program a couple of times while doing Random House publicity: once with Dr. Seuss and once with Peter Bull, the English actor and author. The night of November 27 I was there in a different capacity. I was the homosexual "friend" of Paul Cliffman and GAA cellmate of Marty Robinson. They were to discuss gay liberation, as opposed to the Cat in the Hat and teddy bears.

When Paul and I arrived, we were ushered backstage to the green room. Marty, we were told, was in makeup, and Paul would be touched up in a minute or two. I wondered what they'd do to Paul. The current Paul look was bottom half of face covered by full beard, hair thick on top falling over forehead, and glasses.

Marty emerged pancaked and sprayed, looking pancaked and sprayed, zippy in his lambda T-shirt, calm and grinning like a Cheshire cat. Paul went to makeup, but exited two minutes later saying that they put makeup around his eyes.

Dick Leitsch, executive director of Mattachine managed to get on the show under the pretext that Mattachine, too, represented the homosexual society, albeit a more conservative element. That element demanded to be heard. Marty was particularly upset about Leitsch's appearance, which he thought might fuck up his chances of making points, especially in the area of Lindsay and police harassment. (Leitsch let it be known on several occasions that he was on good terms with Lindsay and thought the mayor was a friend of the gay community.) Paul and Marty, prior to the program, decided that they would not hassle with Leitsch but rather avoid him whenever possible.

They avoided him in the green room. Leitsch emerged from twenty-five minutes of makeup and plopped himself down on a cozy chair, his lover by his side. He was dressed in a yachtsman's jacket, Fire Island sportsy, a definite contrast to the Youth of Today image projected by Marty and Paul.

James Earl Jones, star of *The Great White Hope*, sat quietly, invisibly to the left of Leitsch. Shortly before the program began, Phyllis Diller screamed in. She was dressed in green from head to toe, every single stitch of clothing. She wore a diamond the size of an ostrich egg. Her smile ran from ear to ear. And she was terrifyingly attractive.

"Hi there, James Earl Jones," she said. "I nearly sat on your leg. This is a very nice room. It's a good shape, ha ha ha ha ha ha."

Dick Leitsch ha ha ha'd along, and introduced himself to the green lady. They talked about the Purple Onion in San Francisco. "The guy who owned it was a Barrymore," said Phyllis. "Oh, really?" said Dick Leitsch. "The hungry i means the hungry intellectual," said Phyllis. "Oh, really?" said Dick Leitsch.

Dick Cavett came in. "Phyllis, your shoes are a technicolor dream."

Phyllis ha ha ha'd her reply.

"I'm going out there to alienate the audience now," said Cavett.

"It's a nice room," said Phyllis Diller, and Dick Leitsch shook with laughter.

The moment of truth arrived. Our eyes were glued to the big color television set in the room. The credits appeared: Paul Cliffman and Marty Robinson. We smiled at each other. Dick Cavett started his monologue. Phyllis Diller played with her hair. I scrutinized Leitsch's face and took notes. He knew what I was doing and gave me a dirty look. I stopped. Cavett made one of his New York jokes. "I don't get it," said Phyllis Diller. One of the stage hands called Phyllis to come out. "It's my period," she said, "ha ha ha ha ha ha ha ha." And a moment later she was on TV, a hop, skip, and jump into a zillion homes.

A game of musical chairs was played in the green room. Marty switched from the couch to Diller's chair. Leitsch got up and moved away from Marty. I shifted to a position on the floor. Resettled, we listened to Diller's jibes about being on a non-smokers' cruise, and we cracked up at her references to her unique beauty. We sat through a commercial for Aspergum, and wished James Earl Jones luck as he left the green room for the set. Jones rapped about his Off Broadway play, about Jack Johnson the prizefighter, about Cassius Clay. Dick Leitsch was smoking furiously and pacing up and down the room. He sprang to the door when the three names were called. Paul kissed me. I wished all of them luck, then moved over to the seat next to Leitsch's lover.

Cavett began with "The subject of homosexuality still upsets some people. We will try to discuss it reasonably, but if it's going to give you apoplexy, for heaven's sakes don't watch." He was cautious, but as the program shaped and formed, Cavett loosened up. "What kind of oppression have you suffered?" he queried. Paul replied that he had stones thrown at him for holding a lover's hand, walking down the street (this was news to me—what lover?), and went into the police harassment bit on Forty-second Street, noting that he had himself been arrested for acting as an observer.

Marty, too, talked oppression: "If I were an alien, I wouldn't dare tell you, because I would be deported immediately for being a homosexual. If I applied for a job, I might not get it. Don't think people can't find out that you're a homosexual if they want to. You can go to a private investigating agency and get that information on anyone."

Paul discussed the publishing agency where he had worked during the summer of 1966 (I got him the job) and its special code to pinpoint homosexuals and blacks— this in spite of the existence of fair employment laws. "We face a cruel alternative," Paul continued. "If we deny our emotions and appear straight, then we have a career. But if we live openly and show our affections the way heterosexuals do and lead an open sexual life, then our careers are ended. We feel it is repressive, unfair, and unjust that we face that alternative. There is no reason why we can't be full people, both economically and in terms of our feelings."

Cavett replied by stating many homosexuals have fitted into society and would prefer that homosexuality be a side

162

issue to their personalities. Marty, wisely and beautifully, answered that those of us who do fit into society do so at a great personal price. "Even in the movement, some people are willing to face the government before they'll face their own mothers and say 'Hi, Mom, I'm gay.' "

(A sideline excursion on this issue: Paul's parents had not known about his homosexuality. After the program was taped, he came back to my apartment, where he phoned long distance to tell his mother that he'd be on the Cavett show that night. He believed that his parents, seeing their son in the company of such well-known celebrities as James Earl Jones and Phyllis Diller, would be less likely to feel "shame." Coming clean to his parents was Paul's last barrier. The surprise part was that this man who could literally slay dragons was queasy about calling home. About a week after the program he received a letter from his mother. It wasn't "We forgive" or "Let's discuss" or "How did it happen?" but "Why do it on television and embarrass the neighbors?")

Cavett introduced Dick Leitsch. The word "oppressive" bothered him. "Judges tell homosexuals they're criminals, ministers tell them they're sick, and I'm afraid that these people are going to make them feel oppressed by telling them over and over that they are oppressed."

Cavett, at that point, switched the focus of the program back to the "radical" element. Paul stated, "The Irish and the blacks have found that if they group together into political power groups they get results. We feel that we, too, have to come out politically, as a political power bloc, one feared by the government. Until we are feared by the government, we'll never have our rights. Until we have power, we'll never be free."

Cavett continued, "It seems to me that if you were an actor like James Earl Jones, you'd have more in common with him as an actor than with a busboy who happened to be a homosexual. Isn't it what you've made of yourself that's important?"

"If James Earl Jones were a homosexual, which he is not," Paul began.

"How do you know?" Jones retorted. "And besides, I don't think it's important. I think homosexuality is just another way of achieving love and affection that you didn't get or you don't have." This drew considerable laughter from the panel and a round of applause from the studio audience.

The discussion turned to political tactics. Marty talked about the recent election campaign and the politicians who spoke out on gay rights. He laced into Lindsay and the fact that he'd never spoken out.

"He hasn't spoken out," Dick Leitsch conceded, "but he's done things. Now if you're going to get someone, get Rockefeller. He hasn't spoken out or done a damn thing."

"Strange bedfellows make politicians," joked Cavett as he stopped the show to pause for a commercial.

Cavett then picked up Marty's earlier remark about mothers and raised the question of parental attitudes toward having gay children, mentioning the Joseph Epstein article in *Harper's*.

"A point really offensive to me," said Paul, "was Epstein's statement that homosexuality was a curse that should be wiped off the face of the earth. If someone had said that about the Jews or blacks, *Harper's* would have been burned to the ground. The fact that he said it about homosexuals was left unnoticed by the liberal press, by politicians, by any spokesman in society."

"I can say to Mr. Epstein," Marty added, "that my own personal experience as a homosexual is that of a happy human being. That my homosexuality is one of the assets of my life. I like my life style. I love my lover. I'm happy being what I am. I don't see why Epstein should be trying to define how I should grow up. Rather, when his children grow up, he should wish them happiness and fulfillment in life. If I have those things, I don't see why he should have that attitude."

The segment lasted forty-five minutes. At the finish of the program there was a feeling of pride and accomplishment. We talked to Cavett and Phyllis Diller and to the friends in the audience who came backstage to offer congratulations. Then we were hustled out of the studio through a complicated route which was not the normal backstage exit. Later we discovered that there were people in the studio audience who were waiting outside the stage door to beat up Paul and Marty.

I guess that meant the show was a success.

E<small>BEN AND</small> Cary and I and another "Eben supporter" met for brunch on a Sunday afternoon to discuss Eben's election campaign. Wearing his red shoes, looking like Jesus Christ from the ankles up, like Judy Garland in *The Wizard of Oz* from the ankles down, Eben delighted us with tall tales about his apprenticeship at the Pasadena Playhouse in California and his adventures as a sales clerk at Tiffany's. We got some serious business done, too, between stories.

"I was told I had to have 'planks,' " said Eben. "My 'planks' are the people—the general membership of GAA." As for "platforms," Eben conceded that there were three important issues he'd stress if elected. The first was GAA's failure to communicate with other groups in the city. By opening channels of communication with GLF and Mattachine and STAR and the university groups, Eben hoped that GAA would become less of an elitist organization and relate more to the community it claimed to represent. Eben's second platform was to push GAA into relating to itself. By and large, the individual members had no idea of the meaning of liberation. Eben suggested that we initiate the consciousness-raising methods used by GLF and Women's Liberation. "Let's find out why some of our members can't relate to transvestism, for instance, or anal sex or women." The third issue is that GAA form a gay power bloc in New York City, a bloc that would take in all Manhattan, that would not confine itself to the Village area. "We have a starter with Tony Olivieri," said Eben. "Now let's hit other areas. Let's move into Queens."

The GAA 1970 election committee (a committee for EVERYTHING!) voted to have nominations December 10, elections December 17. The person making a nomination would be allowed three minutes to laud his candidate. The candidate himself would be allowed fifteen minutes for his acceptance and direction speech—part of that time allocated to a question and answer period from the floor. All of the candidates for all of the offices were in the process of sifting out potential nominating speechmakers. Ideally, the nominator would complement his candidate by having the support of a segment of the membership that would not normally support the candidate himself.

The question of who was to make Eben's speech arose. I told Eben that I'd like to do it, and that I was tempted to do it, but there was the problem of my relationship with Paul. Cary said that he would deliver the speech, but there was an "if." "I've got a lot of things I'd like to say about GAA and I may run for the presidency myself. Not that I expect to win it, but running for office would give me an opportunity to say what's on my mind." So we left it there. Cary would probably give the nominating speech, and Eben would pitch for the presidency on the three platforms.

I felt that Eben's chances of winning were slim, but possible. The people who'd vote for him were those who were disgusted with some of Jim and Marty's tactics and policy-making decisions, and those who weren't into Paul's cold approach, logic, and radical politics. Eben was the humanistic, in-between choice. He had the support of some of the fair tax people, the news committee, and the police power committee. The street people didn't know him; they'd support Paul. Eben was also too radical-middle for the Owles-Robinson element. The tactic was to get Eben to small committee meetings. Expose Eben to the membership on an individual basis. That way he'd have a fighting chance.

We missed a Thursday meeting because of the Thanksgiving holiday. The meeting held a week prior to nomination night was monumentally dull. In his presidential report Jim Owles said that a letter was sent to NBC complaining about a segment of a Bob Hope special—an offensive parody on gay liberation in which Hope camped his way through sissy power. GAA was demanding equal time from the network. Jim reminded us that a "Mediazap" dance was scheduled for the following evening at St. Peter's Church and that Young Lord squatters—"really a great bunch of people"—were at the church. They were willing to cooperate with us and move out for the night, but help was needed to remove sleeping bags and bunks from the dance floor area. In the announcement period, Rabbi Herbert Katz reported on a gay synagogue service he was holding in Brooklyn Heights on Friday nights. "This is a reformed synagogue, and the services are in English. Please try to come." And a new committee was set up to search for a permanent loft or clubhouse.

There was an undercurrent of politicking throughout that meeting. The next-to-last roundup. Some candidates made glowing speeches about irrelevant non-issues and smiled graciously at people they despised. If there were babies to be kissed, they'd have been kissed. Asses were kissed, instead.

Afterward Morty Manford openly polled the membership. His unofficial consensus, which he happily brought back to Paul, was that the presidential vote was divided between Jim Owles and Paul, with little support for Eben. Paul was positive that night that he had the presidency. With the Cavett show behind him, with an article about him scheduled for the New York *Post,* and with the prospect of a brilliant acceptance speech next week, there was no doubt in his mind that he'd carry the majority vote. It was a closed issue.

Don Clark called me the first week of December. He would give his last Natural Man Encounter Group Workshop the coming weekend, before moving to the West Coast. He had room in his group for one or two people. He'd take them on a cost-free basis. Do I know anyone who might qualify?

I called Cary. He jumped at the opportunity. Forty-eight hours of group dynamics and psychodrama. Dynamite. Before he left, I visited his apartment and was given instructions on the feeding and walking of Pluto. Cary's parting shot was "I'm almost certain that I'll run for office, but I'll have a definite answer when I return on Sunday."

MEDIAZAP DANCE.
Friday, December 4, 9 P.M. St. Peter's Church. All Welcome. The Mediazap Dance is to note the exclusion of campaign statements on gay rights from *The New York Times* and the bigoted jokes of Bob Hope on NBC-TV. It marks GAA's determination to see justice as it was done by forcing an appearance on the Dick Cavett Show, and zapping *Harper's*

Magazine, in response to anti-gay slander. Out of the closets and into view—MEDIA PENETRATION!

Gay Activists Alliance

And once again, we danced the gay lib blues.

I had dinner with Ralph Hall that night. Ralph, who used to write for *Gay Power,* was now writing articles for *East Village Other.* He asked me over to discuss the misdirection of gay liberation in New York. "There's a whole gray area that's not covered by the Gay Liberation Front or Gay Activists Alliance," said Ralph. "It's an area of community. I feel that we do not need a GAA movement per se but a gay movement and GAA is forgetting or is somehow innocently ignorant of the fact that they hold many gay people's welfare at stake by making organizational rather than community decisions. GAA could do much to drop their political pants for a moment and address themselves to humanness and to their brothers and sisters who are earnestly attempting to create a community of all gay people."

I said to Ralph that there were several people at GAA waiting for a travel agent to book them into the gray area of community. I suggested that he give the organization another try (he used to attend meetings regularly), and Ralph promised he'd come to Candidates' Night.

Ralph started a fire going in his fireplace. He took out a sawed-off pipe. We smoked his powerful grass. Tons of it. And left for the Mediazap dance stoned out of our minds. En route we met Michael Morrissey and some of his friends. They were on mescaline, and the crew of us floated in on a cloud, weaving our way in and out of the music. Our feet never touched ground.

Paul was there. I danced a couple of slow numbers with him. Eben was there. I danced a couple of far-out numbers with him. Ron Diamond was there. I don't remember what I danced with him, but I danced with him. And I swayed around the room with Michael, and Santana'd with Morty Manford, and tapped with Augusto of the news committee and fox-trotted with Frank Thompson of Thompson Galleries and followed-the-leader with the GLF contingent and smoked grass in a corner of the room and drank in every note of music that blasted from the sound system—music that found a quick release through every pore of my body.

We stayed late, until the dance was over and the squatters had returned to claim their sleeping quarters. Paul volunteered to clean up. He and a few faithfuls spic-and-spanned the place until it was shiny new. Eben had the use of Marty Robinson's truck and offered to drive the clean-up squad back to our respective apartments. We sat on cases of beer and soda pop in the back of the truck, tired and dizzy, people not politicians, after the ball.

Too hepped up to sleep, Paul and I talked until the sun came up, and I chose that morning to throw the bombshell.

"I may make Eben Clark's nominating speech."

Paul's voice went high and threatening. "You do that and it's the end of our relationship."

There was a long pause from me. Finally, "Why?" My voice was quivering. "I would nominate Eben, not attack you. Is that so terrible?"

"If you nominate Eben, it will mean to the membership that something is wrong with me."

"Are you saying that the presidency means more to you

than our relationship?" I asked, knowing full well it did. "Yes."

Paul proceeded, calmly and coldly, to say that he would let it be known that my support of Eben was an act of vengeance. He would publicly state that we had a fight and that I was getting back at him through politics. If that didn't work, he would withdraw from the election and concede his vote to Jim Owles. Up to then, Paul claimed he'd support Eben if it was evident before nominating night that he, Paul, would not win. Paul disagreed vehemently with Jim Owles's politics and knew him to be a lousy administrator.

In back of my head I may have expected this response, but when it came, it threw me. I questioned Paul about his conscience insofar as the Owles vote. I questioned him about slandering me to win his political fight. And long into the morning I questioned myself about the past validity of our relationship.

Out of disgust I told Paul I would not nominate Eben. I really didn't know what I would do. The reality of where I now stood with Paul overwhelmed the election issue. I, too, was a political pawn in Paul's chess game of power and politics—a key piece whom he was willing to sacrifice in a manipulative move to win. The problem was, his key piece wasn't carved out of ivory. But it was no longer carved out of Jello, either.

It's difficult to sort out the few days that followed, the days leading to December 10, the day of the nominations. Holly Woodlawn, the transvestite star of Andy Warhol's *Trash*, phoned that Saturday, waking us up from the two or three hours' sleep we had. I had left messages for Holly at the Warhol Factory—in fact, all over town—about a possible *Voice* article. Out of the blue the phone rang. "Can I come over?" Holly said. "I'm at Larry Rivers' apartment. I can be at your place in fifteen minutes."

In twelve minutes Paul up and left, and in twenty minutes Holly arrived and I spent the day with him. We went to see *Trash* (his thirtieth time, my second), sat in the last row of the theater, where Holly guzzled wine and fell asleep. After, we charged through town on nervous energy, hitching rides in the rain, stopping every half hour or so for drinks, dancing at an East Village birthday party, and finally being kicked out of a chi-chi uptown apartment house simply for being Holly Woodlawn and Arthur Bell, such as we were. Freaky and zonked, I took notes along the way, and came out with a terrific story— participator and observer—that hit page one of the *Voice* the following week.

Holly took me temporarily away from myself. Alone, reality came back full blast. I was unable to sleep, and could not deal with what was happening. I wanted far away for a while. I needed rest. I took a few Nembutals and woke up seven or eight hours later and took a few more. Sometime late Sunday night I was awakened by hammering at the front door. It was Cary. He had just returned from the encounter group, said he tried phoning, there was no answer. The sight of me, drugged and incoherent, frightened him. I suppose he got in touch with Eben. I remember eating Chinese food while lying on the floor of Eben's apartment, but I don't remember how I got there or how I got home, whether it was that night or the following day.

There was a lot of Holly and Cary and Eben in the two

or three days that followed. Holly didn't know Paul, didn't know from nothing, but took me under his wing. One night Cary and Eben and Holly and some of Andy Warhol's superstars went to a *Free Time* taping for educational television, and some of us went for drinks after, and it was happy and light, but the Paul threat lingered and confused and saddened and continued to interfere with my sleeping and appetite. I saw Paul the evening before the GAA nominations. We went to the movies and dined at a little Greek restaurant. I could barely look at him. We avoided talking politics or elections or GAA. We couldn't talk feelings. So we hardly talked at all.

Cary called the following morning. He said that Michael Morrissey would nominate him for president. He read me his election speech.

That evening I gussied up in a tux. For kicks I wore an embroidered shirt cut to the belly button, and a choker around the neck. Larry Rivers, the artist, had invited Holly and me to his opening at the Marlborough Gallery. Holly and I planned to go there first, then attend the GAA meeting. Holly wanted to stay at GAA just long enough to hear Eben's speech and to tell him he loved him.

The Rivers show was typical New York. Few people paused long enough to notice art, but did pause to see who was there with whom, wearing what. Holly looked sensational in a Joan Crawford evening gown, circa 1938, and outshadowed the Rivers sculptures. He was the darling of the photographers and ate up every minute of it. By 8:30 we left the show and hitchhiked to the Church of the Holy Apostles. We "entranced" in time for Eben's nominating speech. It was being given by Jean De Vente, who had discarded her standard baseball shirt and slacks for a tan dress—the first time the membership had seen her dressed in what she called "feminine drag." She was wearing the drag out of respect for Eben, and claimed she was also wearing a girdle. Very uncomfortable.

Jean's nominating speech did not laud Eben's character and accomplishments. Instead, Jean did a surprise attack on Marty Robinson. She said she first met Marty at a pleasure committee meeting, a meeting where Marty screeched, "You motherfuckers. Things are going to be run my way or no way at all." Jean recalled that Marty tried to physically attack a member of the street theater committee at a Thursday night meeting. "He can't do things like this," she said. "If it was me, I'd have broken his back." She finished her speech by noting that a vote for Jim Owles was actually a vote for Marty Robinson. And, almost as an afterthought, she said, "We want to draft Eben Clark for president."

Eben was taken aback. He had envisioned Jean's nominating speech, and his own platform speech, as "low key." He decided to talk on a calm level anyway. He approached the table at the front of the room and perched half of his body on it. He wore his red shoes and his red and white argyle socks, his torn Levi's with a *soupçon* of ass peeking through, and a red spaghetti strap and shirt over a brown cotton shirt. His glasses appeared more horn-rimmed than usual. His hair was long and silky.

He began by saying it was sad that things had reached such a bad point that what Jean had just said had to be said. There are a great many voices within the organization that are crying to be heard and are not being given an opportunity to speak. Jean's was one of them. When he accepted the draft, Eben said, people told him he must have planks. He pointed to the membership and said, "Each and every person in this room is my plank." He talked about communicating with other gay groups in the city. He stressed that what we did should have community value, as opposed to GAA publicity value. He said that the organization had to be open to the entire city of New York, rather than have it Village based, and suggested that we try to form a power bloc of gay voters. He asked how many people in the room thought that they were liberated. Approximately one-third of the members raised their hands. He said that the first line of the Gay Activists Alliance preamble reads, "We as liberated homosexual activists . . ." How could we state this when there was a failure on behalf of the organization to find liberation?

Eben received a hearty round of applause. Holly went to kiss him, tripping over dozens of feet, upsetting several minutes of the nominating speech for Paul Cliffman. The speech was being given by a last-minute substitute for Sylvia, who had a change of heart and neglected to make the meeting that night.

The person making Paul's nominating speech did a good job. When it came Paul's turn, he, too, plopped himself in a half-on-the-table-half-off position. He was tense. His speech sounded as if it was carefully rehearsed or memorized. Fundamentally his planks weren't different from Eben's. One exception: Paul came down hard on making GAA a national organization. But he also talked about relating to the community, and my ears pricked. When did he relate? I raised my hand during the question and answer period and asked Paul to explain exactly how he related to the community. He tried to make a joke of it.

"Let's keep our lovers' quarrels off the floor," he said. It was the first time he had openly recognized me as his lover at a GAA meeting. He did not answer my question, and I wouldn't let it go. I said that Paul was not at Weinstein during the entire sit-in week. Paul retorted by blaming me for conflicting information on Weinstein events. Before I was able to answer his allegation, someone else was called, a conservative member who queried Paul on whether he'd change GAA from a non-violent to a violent organization if elected president. Paul answered that at present GAA was too small; it would be ridiculous for us to be violent, except when attacked.

Paul's speech got only a moderate round of applause. He returned to his seat next to Morty Manford. I could only see the back of his head.

Jim Owles appeared next. His speech was a hymn to noncommittal. It was devoid of passion or life. He implied that he had done a good job in the past and would continue to keep us together. He touched on the Natasha incident, and lied. He said that when it happened, he contacted all of the people involved before making a decision. He also touched on "community." He was asked about his relationship with Marty, and if any of Jean De Vente's comments were true. He denied the allegations, saying he was his own man.

He took credit for protecting the people of GAA on the march of Forty-second Street. Then he was asked what he thought were the three most important qualities of a human being. He laughed a nervous laugh and made a feeble attempt to answer. One: self-respect. Two: integrity. He couldn't think of a third.

Michael Morrissey, in the evening's surprise move, said quickly and flatly, "I'd like to nominate Cary Yurman for president."

Cary slowly walked to the main table. He carried his speech in his hand. He put on his granny glasses. And he read:

"I am running for the presidency of GAA for two reasons. First because I would like to see GAA take on a new direction in the upcoming year, and second because I'd like to see GAA taken out of the hands of people who are not worthy of the trust of the membership."

Cary said that, for the most part, GAA had failed. He claimed that the organization had been unable to stop police harassment, unable to effect changes in laws, unable to bring about any substantive success in liberating homosexuals, and that it had become fragmented within itself. He put the blame on GAA's basic philosophy and tactics. ". . . leading the community into believing that true change will result from political change will lead to disillusionment. After political change has been effected, the people will find their lives unchanged. . . . Political change in the end will achieve very little."

Cary reasoned that the removal of the oppression of the homosexual society of itself is the most important part of gay liberation. "Until homosexuals can relate to each other as human beings and not as sex objects, gay liberation will not be achieved. Until sex is an expression of affection and communication between people, liberation will not be achieved. Impersonal sex will gradually disappear, not because we no longer have the opportunity, but because we are capable of far more rewarding and fulfilling experiences. We will not want to treat other people as objects any more than we will enjoy being treated as objects. And with this change, the quality of the life of each homosexual will be improved. Once gay people have liberated themselves, the rest of society will have no choice but to adjust to the beauty of homosexuality."

Cary then went into personalities. "I feel it is of the utmost importance to all of the members of the organization to know something about the individuals who are asking to lead the organization for the next year.

"Marty Robinson is not a candidate for president, but it is Marty Robinson who has led the organization for the past year. Jim Owles has served as a puppet president. The Robinson-Owles team has brought the organization to the brink of disaster each time the organization attempted to disagree with them. Throughout the summer, groups within GAA were purged. The social committee under Phil Raia's chairmanship was abolished because it did not please the Robinson-Owles team. Transvestites were made to feel unwelcome, not as a policy of GAA, but as a result of the Robinson-Owles leadership team.

"I cannot support Marty Robinson, because his methods are opportunistic. GAA disavowed the riots in the Village last August. Yet it was GAA under Marty Robinson who went to the Village Independent Democrats to make political gain for GAA out of a situation it had totally disavowed. GAA under Marty Robinson is a nonviolent political organization that tries to make political gain out of other people's violence. Again Marty Robinson tried to opportunistically take advantage of a sit-in at NYU last fall. When GAA's name was mentioned at the sit-in, it was roundly booed. GAA's isolation from the community reflects Marty Robinson's. Marty Robinson has become the

Dick Leitsch of GAA. The membership of GAA may choose to follow the Robinson-Owles team for another year, but in so doing it should be cognizant of what this team represents.

"Paul Cliffman is also a candidate for president. I did not support him, because I believe he has very little understanding of people, and very little concern of human needs. He believes people should be led and they will follow unthinkingly. I do not agree with him and I did not support him. But Paul Cliffman has done something which I believe disqualifies him from serious consideration as president of GAA.

"Beneath his oratory, Paul Cliffman is a political animal in the worst sense of the word. He will stop at nothing to achieve his personal aims. And it is this flaw in his character which I believe disqualifies him to be president of GAA.

"Let me give you an example of what I mean. Arthur Bell, who has been in love with him for six years, supports Eben Clark for president. When he told Paul Cliffman that he was going to nominate Eben Clark, Paul Cliffman told Arthur Bell it would be the end of their relationship and that furthermore he would let it be known that Arthur Bell's support of Eben Clark was the result of Paul Cliffman breaking up the relationship and that Arthur Bell was supporting Eben Clark simply to be vindictive. Cliffman was willing to smear the integrity and reputation of a man who loved him because he would allow no one and nothing to stand in his way. I bring this episode to the attention of the membership because it is an outrage. It is certainly within the bounds of an election to discuss the character of the candidates, and it is the character of Paul Cliffman I want the membership to understand.

"Eben Clark is also a candidate for president. He has been chairman of the police power committee. He has a sense of the community and a feeling for people. I respect him.

"I am also a candidate for president. I know I will be criticized for being as candid as I have been. But I have been in GAA a long time, and I feel it is time the truth were stated openly and some fresh air was let into the organization. If the truth hurts, it cannot be helped. I cannot stand silently by and do nothing about what happens to this organization."

Cary's speech was greeted with boos and hisses. Many members laughed, many were shocked by Cary's audacity to name names and delve into personal issues. The first part of his speech about the direction of the movement was lost. Most of those members present believed that GAA could do no wrong, and they closed their ears to criticism. As Cary talked about Paul's lack of concern regarding human needs, Paul frantically motioned with his hand. He would not be recognized by the chair. Paul bobbed up and down and finally said, "This man is a liar." He turned to the membership and said Cary was attacking his character and he had to defend himself. Then, looking at Cary, he asked, "Isn't it true that you've been living as Arthur Bell's lover for three months?"

Paul Cliffman, liberated Paul Cliffman, doing a cuckolded-lover routine. What a joke. Paul Cliffman fighting for his political life.

The accusation came as a below-the-belt punch to me,

just as I suspect Cary's speech of enlightenment came as a shocker to Paul. In retrospect, I should have said, So what if it's true? I should have said, I wish it were true. I should have said, Fuck you, Paul Cliffman, fuck you. I didn't. I ran to the speakers' table, where Cary was shaking his head, and shouted loud enough to be heard in the bell-tower, "That's a lie. It's typical of your manipulative tactics. Everything that Cary said in his speech is true. Every single word."

Paul's eyes shot around the hall. He had overplayed his hand. He said his integrity had been questioned and he'd withdraw his nomination for the presidency.

At that point I left the church with three or four people, including Cary. I had made the break. I had liberated myself from the political animal that I loved and resented. I was free from Paul Cliffman. There was no one waiting in the wings now, but myself.

We went to a party at Larry Rivers' loft. The Andy Warhol crew were present, along with a couple of hundred professional New Yorkers. Holly, in a corner, was doing a tango with his facial muscles. He asked me to sit on his lap, played mama to my baby, until I got too heavy. Cary and I soon isolated ourselves from the madness around us to discuss the madness we had just left. We smoked hash. Grass. More grass. The room, everything, spinning, the evening, the week, everything. Near me, the white-lipped women, the pony-tailed men, enormous sculptures hailing the age of the motorcycle and hypodermic needle. I wondered if I died a week ago. Was I dancing my way through Hades? Mother, God, Holly, Paul,

Cary, take me somewhere. Take me somewhere. Don't leave me alone.

The following day Michael Morrissey and I dropped mescaline. It was a first for me. Fuzzy control. Fine. We visited the Metropolitan Museum of Art and talked to the statues. We window-shopped and I bought Michael tons of jade, locked up in glass cases, circa a million years B.C. We held on to each other, tripping down that *Hello Dolly* stairway, past those gorgeous Rodins, each of whom or which was propositioned. We discussed committing sodomy at the fountain pool, as a public relations gesture for gay liberation.

Along the tripway we stopped for pineapple temptation sundaes, and I remember telling Michael that he must eat healthier foods because he was heavily into drugs, and the couple at the next table said, "Yes, you should eat soup if you're heavily into drugs." We visited Eben, who told us of a hairy phone call from Paul accusing all of us of conspiracy. It didn't matter to Eben, and it didn't matter to me, not at all, except that I had to clutch Michael, in fact, crawl into his humanness, there on Eben's floor where I was spending too much time of late.

Friends of Eben's came over, and Michael and I came down from our trip. Eben guided us; we played *Imitation of Life*. Each person in that room assumed a character. Eben, I think, was Lana, and someone else was Sandra Dee, and Michael was John Gavin, and we did a whole interrelations shtick that was beautiful and funny and right.

Michael and I hitchhiked back to his downtown apartment. He and his roommate packed an overnight bag and moved in with me for a few days. We did the freedom bit. Lots of dancing, lots of Holly Woodlawn, walks in the rain, giggling in coffee shops, revelations in front of the fireplace, grass and great vibes.

I went to two GAA committee meetings that week. The first with Cary. The committee on committees, chaired by Pete Fisher. Paul was there. Titanic iceberg time.

We discussed restructuring the mandates of the legal and news and graphics and social committees in an excruciatingly boring manner. All of us put in our two cents (some four cents) on every issue. The *Robert's Rules of Order* clique used parliamentary procedure shit at every opportunity. When one of Paul's motions was defeated, he said, "The assassins are here." The pleasure committee demanded to know if their mandate was to give dances to raise the consciousness of the gay community or to give dances to make a profit for GAA on a regular basis. The air was filled with distrust and hostility and when Paul said that he had, in fact, changed his mind about resigning from running, one of Jim Owles's henchmen referred to *Robert's Rules*, claiming Paul was no longer eligible since he copped out publicly. Whatever Mr. Robert and his rules had to say on this point, Paul would run, integrity be damned.

The "coordinating" committee meeting held the day before election night was *Titanic* revisited. Eleven committee chairmen languished around walnut-stained Livingston Hall at Columbia, two feet away from a Christmas tree and three feet away from a sign reading, "Deck the Halls with Balls of Holly," making me wish that fabulous

Holly was there to add oomph to the deadly proceedings. Pamphleting at election night was brought up and voted down. "There shouldn't be any electioneering at all." And those words again, "according to the constitution, parliamentary procedure, amendment," noose words that were choking GAA, noose words spoken by an archetypical homosexual mother who wouldn't allow her baby to grow up. Mama was strangling baby. Mama couldn't kiss baby goodbye.

The night of the election the place is packed beyond belief. Chairs are lined up differently. They are in groups so that the election committee, sworn and true, can carefully and efficiently collect the ballots by basket with minimum inconvenience. The hall is newly painted, yellow and green. The GAA banner is there above the head table. Lambda, lambda, everywhere. Shirts, sweaters, pins, shopping bags, duffel kits, necklaces, rings, in lambda we trust, all others pay and pay and pay.

Morty Manford, despite the voting down, is distributing a pamphlet at the front door: "An Analysis of the Candidacy for Office of President." He charges Cary Yurman with Agnewism. The pamphlet reads, "I urge you to see beyond the obnoxious rhetoric of the Machiavellians."

"Where did you pick up Machiavellians?" I ask Morty.

He doesn't answer me.

We are handed a GAA election ballot, duly authorized and stamped. The official document gives voting procedures ("Vote for one candidate for each office") and lists the candidates. At the left of the room sit the Eben contingent. The street people are there. Sylvia and Natasha have made a special effort to come out and to bring some of their voting friends. Sylvia tells Eben that he has changed his mind about Paul, and that Eben now has the vote of the street people.

Cary is next to me, Michael Morrissey directly in front, and Eben a row in front of Michael. We are talking among ourselves, a chatty, cheery lot, with not a hope in the world of winning, but plenty of hope.

Paul Cliffman is seated next to Morty, in the center part of the room. "Strained" is a mild word to describe the vibrations from the Cliffman camp. Jim Owles and his people are on the opposite side. Unfortunately, the drama of the week has boomeranged both for Eben and Paul, and now non-Jim Owles supporters claim they'll support Jim. When voting time finally comes, we check in our choices. The election committee leave the room with the filled-in form. They will come back with the results as soon as they are duly counted, recounted, re-recounted, and re-re-recounted. They lock the church door ("A fire hazard," someone shouts) so no infiltrator can mess around with voting sheets. Many of the candidates are shitting in their pants. But with a chin-up approach, they bide their time with committee reports.

A young woman who has been with the organization since the summer hands out a statement: "Someone's Crying to Be Heard." She talks from the floor. "Do you think that because our present constitution is Paul Cliffman's reality, that he might present a new constitution that we related to more naturally? . . . When Jim Owles was president, did you feel good about GAA's relationship to such external realities as STAR? . . . Do you think that while still doing our own GAA thing, we might somehow relate better? . . . Do you get the feeling that Eben Clark can feel his way in a situation unrigidly, while still following our constitution, and help get the good things we want despite our superficial differences?"

Little mind is paid to the young woman. She leaves the floor, crying to be heard.

The moment of truth arrives. The door unlocks. And our version of Price and Waterhouse step in:

Jim Owles, 78 votes
Eben Clark, 30 votes
Paul Cliffman, 20 votes
Cary Yurman, 1 vote

Marty Robinson is popping buttons clapping. Paul runs to Jim and plants a peck on his cheek. Jim gives a "let's all get back together" speech. And Cary wonders who the one vote comes from. "I'm probably the only candidate who didn't vote for himself."

The Eben camp visited my place after the elections. We had a fire going. We smoked. We were glad that it was over. We could relax and be friends.

THE next day I made a raw spinach and mushroom salad for our anniversary party, which I did not attend. Instead I left town for Christmas with my parents in Montreal, a little sad, a little happy, a lot relieved that the elections were over, and that the romance that was had reached its final reel.

Am I liberated now? What a foolish question. How can I be when I still look in the mirror ten or twelve times a day to kid myself about my appearance, when I still equate love with Charles Boyer and Irene Dunne and hope with the Wizard of Oz and paradise with lifeguards at Coney Island, wherever they may be. How can I be when my heart goes pitty-pat on those rare occasions when I see Paul Cliffman, the rat, when I continue to zap John Lindsay, the lamb, when I truly don't give a damn about tomorrow, but give ten damns about today.

Will I ever be liberated? Set free from bondage? Released? Never. Never, ever, ever. But I make a fantastic spinach salad. And sometimes I remember to wash the sand from the leaves.

Epilogue

Five months later, after the Paul blowup, after the start
and finish of a carbon copy "almost" affair with yet another intellectual (a baby Einstein this time, nineteen,
sweet and naïve), I have been asked to tie up the events
of the past year or so with an epilogue. Unfortunately,
sunset endings are for 1939 movies. They're fine, but
they don't work for me. Tieing up is for masochists and
sadists. Flawless if you're into it, depressing if you're not.
What I'm saying is that most of what I want to say is in
the book.

Of course, some important things have happened since:
there was the march to Albany to support the state fair
employment bill, and the zaps planned by Richie Aunateau
and his fair employment committee, which have forced
our good mayor to support the fair employment bill.

There's also the STAR quarters in the East Village—
the most interesting and lively house in New York—rented
by Sylvia and the street transvestites, all of whom managed to survive the winter and are ready to spring forth
on Sheridan Square again; last month's 1940s party featuring the clothes, the music, and the dances of the era,
plus the first appearance of Holly Woodlawn in hot pants,
which didn't have anything at all to do with it; the Liberty
Magazine Ball; Vivian Blaine's smash comeback at the

Tony Awards; the acquisition by GAA of a firestation club-house; and the book that Cary's writing about a homosexual subculture.

But best of all is the Beyonds.

What are the Beyonds? I'll have to go back to a week or two after the elections. Several of us at the time felt stymied by the lack of community and growth in GAA and decided to start a consciousness-raising group of our own. We would meet weekly and talk on a common subject directly related to our homosexual experiences. We would conduct our sessions on a free-flow-of-ideas basis and keep our talks unstructured, away from encounter and group therapy, constructive, into truths.

The sessions worked. We called ourselves the Beyonds.

Cary's a Beyond. So are Michael Morrissey and Eben Clark and Jean De Vente and Sylvia when he can make it, and ten others. We come from different backgrounds, our points of view are never the same, homosexuality is our one common ground. Yet when we talk about lovers and other strangers and parents and cruising and our first sexual encounters, a pattern emerges. We discover that the roots of our experiences are similar, sometimes identical. Guilts, so long personal, are externalized. Internal tumors are realized as societal cancers. It's fascinating, mindblowing, and beyond a shadow of a doubt the best thing that's happened to me in a long, long time.

The Beyonds may be working toward a communal arrangement, and why not? We're in love with each other. We react like a miracle family; the vibes are toward tenderness and unity. We're into homosexual liberation first, gay power second. The power thing comes when we're out there in the street with GAA doing our political number—give me a G, give me an A, give me a Y. Inside the arms of Beyond there's no anger. It's warm and comforting.

I mentioned communal before because it would seem the logical next step in the liberation process for me. Communal, my way, would be living and sharing with the Beyonds in a large loft or apartment in Manhattan. It would be great to build a lovenest for sixteen in a city of eight million and settle down with an Eben to enthrall and a Cary to respect and a Michael to marvel at and a Sylvia to protect.

Sweet Beyond juices, emanating self-respect and self-pride, those little things we want from gay liberation, which ultimately come from ourselves. What a wrapup, if it happens. Still. Beyond. A wrapup, I feel, that will be another beginning in a never-ending process toward self-liberation.